PRIME

PRIME

The Complete Prime Rib Cookbook

John Whalen III

CIDER MILL PRESS

BOOK PUBLISHERS

KENNEBUNKPORT, MAINE

This icon is used throughout to identify recipes that are naturally gluten-free, but be sure to check the labels of your broth, stock, wine, and other packaged ingredients to ensure that your chosen brands do not contain gluten.

13-Digit ISBN: 978-1604335958

10-Digit ISBN: 1604335955

This book may be ordered by mail from the publisher. Please include $4.95 for postage and handling. Please support your local bookseller first!

Books published by Cider Mill Press Book Publishers are available at special discounts for bulk purchases in the United States by corporations, institutions, and other organizations. For more information, please contact the publisher.

Cider Mill Press Book Publishers

"Where good books are ready for press"

12 Spring Street
PO Box 454
Kennebunkport, Maine 04046

Visit us on the Web! www.cidermillpress.com

Design: Jon Chaiet

Photos: Photos courtesy of Peter Kaminsky (page 12), John Whalen Jr. (pages 6 bottom, 8, 124, and 254 bottom); and Amy Paradysz (pages 6 top and 252 top). All other images used under license from Shutterstock.com.

Printed in China

1 2 3 4 5 6 7 8 9 0

First Edition

CONTENTS

AU JUS, SAUCES, AND GRAVIES 127

PRIME TIME

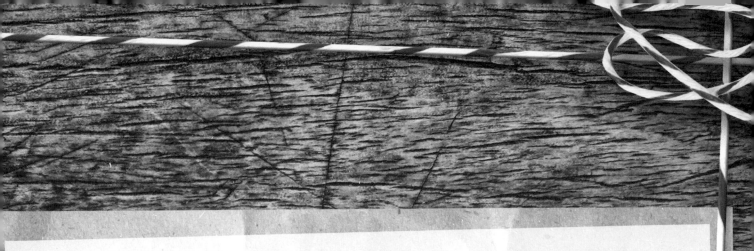

By Peter Kaminsky

What would you serve if Don Draper were coming to dinner at your house?

A three pound lobster?

Too messy.

How about T-bone steak?

Really hard to do right for a dinner party; if you are not a real grill-master you're pretty much guaranteed to overcook some steaks and undercook others.

I wouldn't hesitate a second to come up with my featured entrée on a "Mad Men" menu. Prime rib, on the bone—a big standing roast with a salty, crispy crust and a pink interior done to a perfect 120-medium-rare-degrees. In the same way that a magnum of champagne or a jeroboam of Burgundy announces, "We're getting down to some serious wine drinking now," a prime rib of beef speaks of largesse, of bounty, of pure hedonistic dining. As it was in the days of tailfins on Cadillacs and three-martini luncheons, the prime rib is still the ultimate dinner party meal.

When I was asked to write this introduction, a scene from childhood bubbled up in my memory. I was in my early teens on a road trip with my parents. My dad had a network kiddie show (Pip the Piper) and was doing some appearances at county fairs and the like. We stopped in Boston for a meal at Durgin Park, a time-honored restaurant about which my parents spoke fondly. I ordered prime rib for no other reason than that it sounded impressive. It lived up to its promise, serving up a slab of beef that hung off the end of the plate like one of Salvador Dali's limp watches. That piece of meat is imprinted on my brain like the brand on a prize steer. It was followed by an Indian Pudding dessert (molasses, sugar, corn meal, and butter), which taught me that a full-on prime rib repast is not for the faint of appetite.

Over the years, my palate changed along with America's and I filed prime rib in the drawer labeled "old-fashioned stuff."

That all changed with my first trip to Argentina. My goal was trout fishing, which Argentina affords in abundance, but I was equally thrilled to experience the gaucho's way with meat. They have raised the practice of grilling to a delectable art. In the Patagonian hinterlands, I became friends with South America's most famous chef, Francis Mallmann, who had recently eschewed the fancy food that he had been serving to rich Argentines in favor of wood-fire cookery. One of his crowd pleasers was a whole cow—1,600 pounds—roasted over a pit for fourteen hours. It feeds two hundred people, maybe three hundred. For smaller gatherings, Francis would prepare an *ojo de bife*—literally translated as rib eye, but it was in fact a prime rib roast.

One Christmas, Francis and his family came to our house in Brooklyn for dinner. "I'll bring the meat, you take care of the rest," he said. I was not prepared for the amount of meat he brought—two whole racks of rib roast, about sixty pounds of meat!

"Jesus, Francis," I said. "There's only fourteen of us here. Who in the hell do you think is going to eat all of this?"

"In Argentina, we figure four pounds of meat per person," he answered by way of dismissing my astonishment.

Long story short, we roasted those two racks forever and still they weren't done. My mother suggested that we serve ourselves from the outer parts of the roast and slice the rest up into rib-eye steaks that we could freeze and eat through the winter.

The parts of the meat that we did consume that afternoon were, in a word, supernal. Grass-fed and aged, they had an almost obscene funkiness to them. The inner or "eye" part of each slice was the deep juicy pink of a rain-soaked rose. My favorite part the roast however was—and still is—the outside strip that cups the rib eye and is known as the deckle (Francis calls it the *tapa de bife*). It is well marbled and succulent. People often skip it because it looks well done. Big mistake. I could be content with a serving of nothing but deckle.

At my house, prime rib is now unfailingly the centerpiece of our Christmas dinner. Then for Memorial Day, another one roasted for five of six hours over a smoldering wood fire kicks off grilling season as part of a big backyard *asado*—which is how Argentines say, "More meat than you can ever imagine anyone eating without grafting two more inches on your belt."

Whether you do your prime rib *a la Argentine*—laced with chimichurri, crusted in horseradish, rubbed with cumin and cayenne—or baptized with a merlot gravy, you'll find every possible variation on this fabled cut in this book, along with sides, desserts, and two-fisted cocktails. Or if you're like Don Draper, maybe you warm up with four fingers of one of the dozens of whiskeys the contributors have selflessly pre-tested for prime rib compatibility.

Lest you think you need a special occasion for a prime rib meal, rest assured, as far as your guests are concerned, prime rib *is* the occasion.

PRIME RIB ROAST OVER A WOOD FIRE

By Peter Kaminsky

Although I've written five cookbooks featuring grilling, there's no question that I learned the most from Francis Mallmann. A few years ago he prepared a banquet on a hillside in Uruguay. For those of you unfamiliar with the landscape of this beautiful little country, it's so green it makes you cry. He did a whole lamb, split open, and roasted on an iron cross, along with a 20-pound salmon cased in salt and roasted in a device of his own invention, featuring two levels of fire with the salmon in between. When I showed up at the site in the morning, I noticed two standing rib roasts were placed above a fire so low I could hold my hand just above the grate for a count of "Twelve Mississippis." I had seen roasts done on the grill and even made a few myself, but, as I pointed out to Francis, I had never done one that took nine hours to cook.

"Oh, if you're in a rush you can do it in six," he said. "When you cook it at very low heat for a very long time, you get a beautiful crust and it's uniformly rare all the way through. It's also deliciously smoky."

Don't be put off by the amount of time. As you ready the yard, prep the side dishes, and grill the cuts you will serve to start the meal, it's nice to sit by the fire from time to time and mess around with the coals and the meat. It's also an opportunity to drink a beer or two over the course of the day. And if anyone busts you for sitting around drinking a beer while there's work to be done, simply point out that you are tending to the piece de resistance of the whole meal.

I have since made this rib on special occasions. To keep the fire at a constant temperature, after I place the roast over the smoldering coals, I start another fire that I use to replenish the cooking fire as needed. Keep that second fire going all through the cooking process.

Timing is not exact here. Your sensitivity to heat may be different than mine, and, as a result, the heat of your fire will be different. Air temperature also plays a role. For a four-rib roast, four to six hours is usually right and for a seven-ribber, about six to eight. I serve this as the last part of an Argentine-style meatfest (sausages, sweet breads, cross-cut short ribs, strip steak, lots of grilled vegetables, and potatoes and sweet potatoes buried in the embers).

At the three-hour mark, you can coat the roast liberally with chimichurri. As it begins to crust, re-

---

MAKES 8 TO 15 SERVINGS AS AN ENTRÉE. IF SERVED AS PART OF A MIXED GRILL, MAKES 20 TO 25 SERVINGS.
ACTIVE TIME: 2 HOURS
TOTAL TIME: 6 TO 9 HOURS

1 4- to 7-rib rib roast, 7 to 20 pounds

2 cups Argentinian Chimichurri (see next recipe), for basting

2 cups Argentinian Chimichurri, for serving

peat once or twice until the roast is done.

An instant-read thermometer is indispensible. Remember, big cuts have what is called carryover heat, so the bigger the roast the faster it will cook in the very last—and most critical stages. I remove the roast from the fire when it reaches 115 degrees and let it rest for fifteen minutes before carving. A longer rest won't hurt. Then I separate the entire "eye" from the bones and throw the still-meaty bones back on the fire for the true trenchermen (and trencherwomen) in the crowd to gnaw on. To my way of thinking, a faithful dog also merits a bone.

ARGENTINIAN CHIMICHURRI

MAKES 4 CUPS
ACTIVE TIME: 10 MINUTES
TOTAL TIME: 15 MINUTES

1½ cups red wine vinegar

12 garlic cloves, minced

3 shallots, minced

1½ scallions, minced

3 Fresno chiles, finely chopped (for more spice, substitute a minced habanero)

3 tablespoons freshly squeezed lemon juice

3 teaspoons fresh sea salt

1½ cups flat-leaf parsley, minced

1½ cups fresh cilantro, minced

6 tablespoons oregano, minced

2¼ cups extra-virgin olive oil

By John Whalen III

Used with many types of meats, chimichurri can be used as marinade, though this is sometimes a little risky because of the light kick from the Fresno chile. Serve the chimichurri sauce on the side, and for those who would like even more heat, substitute a habanero in place of the Fresno chile!

1. In a medium bowl, combine the vinegar, garlic, shallot, scallion, Fresno chile, lemon juice, and salt and let rest for 15 minutes.

2. Next, add the parsley, cilantro, and oregano, then gradually whisk in the extra-virgin olive oil. Serve chilled or at room temperature.

THIS ARGENTINEAN CHIMICHURRI SAUCE IS FANTASTIC ALONGSIDE THE B&B PRIME RIB (PAGE 125).

CHEESE, PLEASE

By Lynne Devereux, founding president of
California Artisan Cheese Guild

Handcrafted cheeses offer a delicious way to preserve nature's seasonal bounty. Fresh milk from cows, goats, and sheep that flows freely in spring is captured in the cheeses we enjoy year-round. Creating an inviting cheese platter can be an exercise in spontaneity or a well-planned excursion. I chose just a few favorites from literally hundreds of cheeses for pre- or post-meal delights.

Adding a cheese course will enhance the beefy, earthy, Prime experience as you linger a while longer at the table, savoring all that comes from farms,

good cooking, and sharing food.

A few guidelines to get you started:

How many cheeses

A cheese course can be a single stunning wedge with green olives served before dinner or a slice of blue garnished with honey and toasted nuts for dessert. Typically, a selection of three cheeses is the perfect number to serve before dinner or as dessert.

Diversity

Offer something for everyone with a variety of fresh, aged, mild, and strong cheeses. A mix of milks—cow, sheep, and goat is sure to please. A variety of styles—bloomy rind, washed rind, Cheddar, and blue creates eye-appealing colors and shapes.

How Much to Serve

For a first course or dessert, plan about 2 ounces of cheese per person. If you want a platter with a bountiful look, purchase more than your guests will enjoy. Place the cheeses on a platter in their original form, then cut a few bite-sized wedges or chunks to encourage guests to dive in. Or, make individual plates with beautiful slices and attractive accompaniments on each plate.

Wine Suggestions

Cheese and wine are moving targets and harder to pair than you would think. Go for a strategy of harmony by matching textures—crisp wines with tart, young cheeses and creamy, lush wines with rich, palate-coating cheeses. Choose delicate wines with delicate cheeses and robust wines with full-flavored, complex, and aged cheeses. Surprisingly, white wines are better all-round cheese partners, as are champagne and sparkling wines. Save those big reds for the meaty prime rib course. And don't forget about beer! Craft brews are sure-fire partners for most cheeses and perfect for summer and harvest menus.

Part I: The Starter Course

In the European tradition, a cheese course follows the main course and might precede dessert or end the meal, while Americans are more likely to enjoy cheeses before the meal, with a cocktail or glass of sparkling wine. Accompaniments can be simple—olives or pickled vegetables, nuts, sliced baguette, or interesting crackers and

flatbreads. Keep the accompaniments to a well-chosen minimum that pique the appetite for the meal to come.

Humboldt Fog, Cypress Grove Chevre, California

An iconic soft-ripened goat cheese with a bloomy white rind and a stripe of vegetable ash running through the middle. Humboldt Fog offers a delightful progression of textures from creamy just under the rind to firm at the center. Mildly tangy with a clean, balanced flavor—never goaty or overly salty.

Cabot Clothbound Cheddar, Cabot Creamery, Vermont

A traditional English-style cow-milk farmhouse Cheddar, made by the masters at Cabot Creamery, then wrapped in cheesecloth and transported to the Cellars at Jasper Hill in Vermont to be aged in specially designed caves for ten months. Firm and crumbly, with savory and sweet notes and a snappy, sharp finish.

Louis D'or, Fromagerie du Presbytére, Quebec

An award-winning washed-rind cheese made with raw milk from pastured cows, the style is similar to the great cheeses from the Jura region of eastern France. Large wheels are aged at least nine months to develop complex flavors of fruit, nuts, and brown butter, with a creamy, semi-firm texture.

Taleggio, Italy

One of the oldest soft cheeses from Italy, an aromatic washed-rind cow milk cheese with a golden-orange crust and a semisoft, silky interior. Aromas and flavors are reminiscent of peanuts, beef, butter, and earthy mushroom.

Wensleydale, England

Made by a single creamery in Yorkshire, this cow-milk cheese was originally made by monks in the twelfth century. Made in large, drum-shaped wheels and aged three to nine months, the cheese develops a moist, semi-firm interior and aromas of cheese-cake and caramel with a tart finish.

Manchego, Spain

A traditional sheep-milk cheese with a distinctive basket-weave rind made in large facilities or by smaller, artisanal creameries. Look for artisanal Manchego made with raw milk and aged up to one year. The texture is firm but buttery from the high-fat sheep milk, with a salty, nutty, and mellow flavor.

Part II: The Dessert Course

Think of cheese as the interlude that follows a main course and may or may not lead to a sweet ending. This is the time to open that special bottle of luscious dessert wine or sherry to serve with a selection of rich and creamy cheeses or aged, caramel-y Goudas. Serve with fresh, seasonal fruit, dried apricots, Medjool dates, or figs, and honey or honeycomb. Cheese as the final course will usher your meal to a lingering, satisfied, cheese-drenched bliss. If absolutely needed, follow with chunks of high-quality semisweet chocolate and toasted nuts.

Triple Crème Brie, Marin French Cheese, California

A lush, creamy, soft-ripened bloomy-rind cow-milk cheese made by a creamery founded in 1865 using fresh milk and cream from neighboring family farms. The cheese ripens from the outside, becoming softer and more flavorful. Flavors of sweet milk and butter mingle with earthy mushroom in the rind.

Hudson Valley Camembert, Old Chatham Sheepherding Company, New York

A well-known dairy sheep farm mixes ultra-rich sheep milk and cow milk with a touch of added cream to create this unique cheese. The interior is soft ivory, with a lush, buttery texture, a tart, nutty flavor, and an earthy, white-mottled rind.

Winnimere, Jasper Hills, Vermont

Already a classic American original cheese, Winnimere was developed in 2012 to showcase the rich, high-fat, high-protein winter's milk of the farm's Ayrshire cows. Rimmed in spruce bark and washed in brine as it ripens, the spoonable cheese offers a range of flavors, from smoky bacon to mustard to fruit. To serve, peel away the top rind and let the bark form a bowl for the paste within. (Available seasonally.)

L'Amuse Gouda, Amsterdam

Made in the Netherlands with milk from Holstein Friesian cows, this Gouda is aged in cooler temperatures for two years. The interior is a deep amber color, with the crunch of tiny crystals. Aromas are of hazelnut and caramel, and there's a creamy texture with a nutty, slightly salty flavor and a long complex finish.

Pecorino Toscano, Italy

One of Italy's most ancient cheeses, this sheep-milk cheese is now made by hundreds of producers. As the cheese ages, the rind is dry-salted and massaged with olive oil. Look for cheese aged six months or more with a thin, golden rind and firm interior. Flavors are milky sweet with nut and caramel notes.

Bleu d'Élizabeth, Fromagerie du Presbytere, Quebec

A classic blue-veined cow-milk cheese with beautiful, greenish-blue streaks in an ivory background that's aged sixty days. The texture is moist and creamy leading to fruitiness, balanced salt, and a buttery finish.

CLASSY COCKTAILS

By Carlo DeVito

There is possibly nothing sexier or more adult and suave as going to a steakhouse or restaurant and having a few cocktails before the main attraction. People are usually well dressed, or at least coiffed. It's grown-up time. It was in the days of "Mad Men" and remains ingrained as such today, a part of the Prime experience, whether you're out or at home.

Many of my father's friends were restaurateurs. We could never just walk in and sit down for dinner. You had to first say hello to at least three or four tables of people and have at least one drink at the bar, whether they asked you to wait or not. More often, he would, in his favorite restaurants, order his appetizers at the bar and have them waiting for him at the table when he finally chose to sit down. This way he could hold forth at the bar a while and enjoy.

He thoroughly enjoyed a cocktail or two before sitting down. To him, being at the bar was as much a part of the evening as the actual meal. Dressed in a jacket and tie, and always with a pocket square, he could strike up a conversation with any stranger. He was not intimidated. On the contrary, he was convivial and chatty, and could hold forth on a number of topics. But his best attribute was getting people to talk about themselves. I only understood years later my father was much smarter than me. He could get people going on their favorite subject and more often than not he was thoroughly entertained.

And that was probably the best tip he gave to me about how to act at a bar. Don't talk about yourself to someone else. The way to get them chatting is to have them tell you about themselves.

The classics of the steakhouse remain Martinis, Manhattans, and Negronis. However, today, fueled by the rocket ship that is the craft-distilling boom, mixologists have become the second wave of culinary stars after the chefs. Cocktails are no longer a beverage but an art. And a whole new vision of imbibing has been offered up over the last twenty years. The following section by Amy Zavatto includes a mix of classic cocktails and newer additions for family and friends to savor and enjoy.

The world of whiskies, bourbons, and ryes has exploded. Warren Bobrow's suggestions are a testament to the golden age of craft-distilled spirits. Scottish single malts have remained the ultimate king of the brown spirits world. The bourbons of Kentucky and Tennessee still dominate. And of course, the classic Canadian whiskies have remained popular. But a new cadre of these now comes from as far and wide as California and Oregon, as well as from the Hudson Valley. And rye has made an absolutely spellbinding return.

Cheers!

STEAK-HOUSE SIPPING: 10 CLASSY COCKTAILS

By Amy Zavatto, deputy editor of *Edible Manhattan*

Behind every great meal is a great cocktail. Or, at least, it really should be part of the preamble. But classic steakhouse fare is not the place for fussy molecular mixology—this is where we hearken back to the days of yore, when a drink with more than a few ingredients was looked upon as suspect. As well it should be. Classic cocktails endure because, like a perfectly sizzled porterhouse simply seasoned with salt, pepper, and perhaps a pat of butter or a drizzle of olive oil, they are already perfect.

Take heed, however: You can have the most classic recipe right in front of you, but, just as with a meal, if you don't use good, fresh ingredients, the drink will be a dud. That goes for your vermouth, too, which should always be stored in a cool place (preferably your refrigerator) and not held onto for years on end. If you don't tend to use it up quickly, buy smaller bottles. And as for your spirits, that old chestnut of, "Use the cheap stuff when mixing," is a horrible piece of advice. Use high-quality ingredients, and you and your guests will always drink well. Cheers.

MANHATTAN

2 ounces bourbon
or rye

1 ounce sweet
vermouth

3 dashes Angostura
bitters

1 brandied cherry

In a cocktail shaker filled with ice, pour in all liquid ingredients and stir until thoroughly chilled, about 45 seconds. Strain into a cocktail glass and garnish with the brandied cherry.

DAIQUIRI

2 ounce white rum

¾ ounce fresh lime
juice

½ ounce simple syrup

In a cocktail shaker filled with ice, pour in all liquid ingredients and shake well, about 45 seconds to a minute. Strain into a cocktail glass.

MARTINI

2 ounces gin

1 ounce dry vermouth

1 or 2 green olives or a
lemon twist

In a cocktail shaker filled with ice, pour in all liquid ingredients and stir until thoroughly chilled, about 45 seconds. Strain into a cocktail glass and garnish with the olive or lemon twist.

ROBERT BURNS

2 ounce Scotch

½ ounce sweet vermouth

¼ ounce Benedictine

2 dashes orange bitters

In a cocktail shaker filled with ice, pour in all ingredients and shake well, about 45 seconds to a minute. Strain into an ice-filled rocks glass.

NEGRONI

1 ounce gin

1 ounce sweet vermouth

1 ounce Campari

1 orange twist

Fill a rocks glass with ice. Pour in the gin, sweet vermouth, and Campari. Stir. Garnish with an orange twist.

SOUL KISS

1½ ounces Scotch

½ ounce dry vermouth

½ ounce fresh orange juice

½ ounce Dubonnet rouge

1 orange twist

In a cocktail shaker filled with ice, pour in all liquid ingredients and shake well, about 45 seconds to a minute. Strain into a cocktail glass and garnish with the orange twist.

HANKY PANKY

1½ ounces gin

1½ ounces sweet vermouth

¼ teaspoon Fernet Branca

1 lemon twist

In a cocktail shaker filled with ice, pour in all liquid ingredients and shake well, about 45 seconds to a minute. Strain into a cocktail glass and garnish with a lemon twist.

PRESIDENTE

2 ounce white rum

½ ounce dry vermouth

½ ounce orange curaçao

¼ teaspoon grenadine

1 orange twist

In a cocktail shaker filled with ice, pour in all liquid ingredients and shake well, about 45 seconds to a minute. Strain into a cocktail glass and garnish with the orange twist.

SAZERAC

½ teaspoon absinthe or Pernod

1 sugar cube, or 1 teaspoon sugar

½ teaspoon spring water

3 dashes Peychaud bitters

2 ounces rye

Tilt a rocks glass on a slight angle, and drizzle the absinthe or Pernod into the side. Tilt the glass until it's almost on its side and turn, so that the absinthe coats the inner sides of the glass. Discard any extra absinthe. Drop the sugar cube into the bottom of the glass, wet with the water and bitters, and mash with a wooden spoon or muddler until it breaks apart. Add in 4 or 5 ice cubes and pour in the rye. Stir well.

UP-TO-DATE

2 ounce rye

¾ ounce Manzanilla sherry

¼ ounce Grand Marnier

2 dashes Angostura bitters

1 orange twist

In a cocktail shaker filled with ice, pour in all liquid ingredients and stir until thoroughly chilled, about 45 seconds. Strain into a cocktail glass and garnish with an orange twist.

100 WHISKEYS, SINGLE MALTS, BOURBONS & RYES

By Warren Bobrow, author of *Whiskey Cocktails*

Whiskey, it isn't just for healing any longer. What? Healing? Sure!

During the age of Prohibition, every man, woman, and even your tiny child was permitted a prescription of pure, U.S. government-certified, bottled in bond whiskey. Even Scotch whisky was a long-known cure to what ails ye, at least to the government, which was probably more interested in collecting the taxes on each sale of prohibited liquor, instead of completely eradicating it from the scene. Yes, Scotch and Irish whiskey was available too, but only with a prescription!

Now, after decades of neglect, whiskey is suddenly hot again with craft distilleries popping up all over the United States and seemingly all over the world. Their venerable names are rolling off the tongues of everyone who ever obsessed over their Jack and Coke, when they really should have been drinking scintillating and sophisticated Rob Roy cocktails made with spicy and erudite Canadian whisky.

For the pleasure of eating meat, there really isn't anything more enjoyable than an effervescent tumbler of whiskey, treated to quality mixers and served in a carefully handcrafted cocktail. I should know—it's made me a living. There are hundreds of different types of whiskey and whisky on the market—an explosion in popularity that carries this venerable product around the globe. Even in India the thirst for whisky far outstrips the available grains and it's then distilled from sugar cane, colored and flavored to mimic Scotch. This whisky promises a hangover of massive proportions; quality levels are not so high with this ingredient that's not far from white industrial rum. But where the good stuff comes into play, one of the world's best is Amrut.

In the United States, craft distillation is a rising art and science. Some whiskies are made in huge quantities by factory distilleries, while others harness the grain to glass approach. I'm very fond of new varieties of bourbon and whiskey. These varieties are what they call "orphan" or "lost" barrels, according to some and negotiant to others. These lost barrels have become another income stream to whiskey companies. They in turn enable folks to "make" whiskey without a still because it's not an inexpensive proposition to get into craft distilling.

Up the Hudson River in the Hudson Valley, Tuthilltown Spirits Distillery ages and distills locally grown grain at the distillery. It's then rested in small casks for a minimum of two years to become the more expensive and desirable "straight" whiskey. The distiller has harnessed fermented grains with a license from the government. From here, it may be carefully spun into liquid gold anyplace where distillation has become an art form. Anywhere that's

passionate and wealthy that is, because you don't get into distillation without some real money behind you. And as far as food friendliness goes, there is nothing more exciting than a well-chilled Collins glass filled with ice, Pickett's Ginger Beer Syrup, and Barrell Whiskey. Hey, you can even grace that glass with a splash of seltzer to make your own soda just like a soda jerk, for the whiskey. That drink makes me darned thirsty and I hope it excites your penchant as well.

Whiskey is not just served in a glass without ice like your grandfather drank it any longer. It's highly mixable in cocktails and it's serious fun.

I'm learning more these days about the passion and richness of artisan Canadian whisky. Here are a few that you should try, along with the more commonly known and venerable favorites.

CANADIAN WHISKY

Alberta Premium Dark Horse

Black Velvet (Try it with cane sugar cola)

Crown Royal (Get out the ginger ale)

Hirsch Canadian Rye Whisky

J.P. Wiser's Whisky

Kindilan

Lot No. 40 Whisky

Pendleton 1910

Pike Creek Whisky

WhistlePig

UNITED STATES: BOURBON, RYE, TENNESSEE SIPPING, AND ALTERNATE GRAIN WHISKEY

Anchor Distilling

Baker's

Balcones

Barrell Bourbon and Whiskey

Benjamin Prichard's Tennessee Whiskey

Bomberger's

Booker's

Breuckelen Distilling

Buffalo Trace

Bulleit

Catoctin Creek

Corsair

Dad's Hat

FEW Spirits

Four Roses

George Dickel

Heaven Hill

High West

Hudson Spirits (Tuthilltown)

Jack Daniel's

Jim Beam

Knob Creek

KOVAL

Lost Spirits

Maker's Mark
Middle West Spirits
MGP
Noah's Mill
Old Forester
Old Grand Dad
Old Rip Van Winkle
Pappy Van Winkle
Black Maple Hill
Rock Town Distillery
Rogue Spirits
Santa Fe Spirits
St. George Spirits
Stranahan's Colorado
Whiskey
Tamworth Distilling
Tincup
W.L. Weller
Widow Jane
Willett
Woodford Reserve

SCOTCH (FROM SCOTLAND) WHISKY (NO "E")

Aberlour a'bunadh
Ardbeg
Ballantine's
Balvenie
Blackadder
Bowmore
Bruichladdich (My favorite)
Bunnahabhain
Cadenhead's
Compass Box Whisky

Glenmorangie
Isle of Jura
Lagavulin
Laphroaig
Old St. Andrews
Talisker
Whyte & Mackay
Oh so many more!

INDIAN WHISKY (YES, THEY DO MAKE BRILLIANT WHISKY IN INDIA)

Amrut (World class)
Paul John
Royal Gold (Definitely an acquired taste)

IRISH WHISKEY (YES, THERE IS AN "E" IN THERE, JUST LIKE IN THE UNITED STATES)

Avoca
Bushmills
Clontarf
Jameson
Midleton Very Rare (To dream an impossible dream…)
Powers Gold Label
Redbreast
Teeling
Tullamore DEW
Tyrconnell
Yellow Spot

JAPANESE WHISKY (BEATING THE SCOTS AT THEIR OWN GAME!)

Eigashima Shuzo
Nikka From the Barrel
Nikka Yoichi
Suntory Suntory Hibiki
Yamazaki

GERMAN WHISKY

Edelster Aventinus (Assertive!)
GLINA Whisky Single Grain (Ambitious!)

AUSTRIAN WHISKEY

Hans Reisetbauer (Not what you may expect!)

FRENCH WHISKY

Armorik Breton
Bastille
Brenne (Luscious, kissed by sunshine, cut herbs, and sweet honey)
Glann ar Mor
Guillon

STARTERS, SOUPS, AND SALADS

Starters, soups, and salads are some of the most fundamental elements to a classic prime rib dinner. Starters, such as beefsteak tomatoes with balsamic vinaigrette, chorizo-stuffed mushrooms, or shrimp cocktail, stand alone from the rest of the meal. Just choose what you and your guests will enjoy, keeping an eye on what's fresh in season.

With soups, you always want to begin by sweating your vegetables and seasonings so that you then build upon strong flavors. Often, you'll need to use a stock, which is a very time-consuming process that involves boiling your meat's bones for a long period of time, letting the marrow seep out. If you do not have the time for the stocks, you can simply purchase premade stock at your local supermarket or farmers market. With salads, you'll always want to choose the freshest and most in-season vegetables at your local farmers' market. For myself, I always appreciate a nice arugula salad with cucumbers and cherry tomatoes, topped with a nice vinaigrette. A vinaigrette is composed of equal parts extra-virgin olive oil and vinegar; add a couple herbs and citrusy flavors and you've got the perfect dressing for the summer.

Speaking of summer, grilling is the way to go with your soups. Soups and grilling are rarely paired together, but when they are they produce the best and most flavorful meals. Preparing soups over the grill will take time and frequent attention—and, when using a charcoal grill, that means restocking the coals about every hour. When making soup and salad toppings like charred bacon on the grill, it is extremely important to find a quality charcoal that will give you the perfect mix between smoke and heat. In addition, be sure to have several cups of presoaked hickory or oak woodchips alongside the grill to toss onto the coals when needed.

There's just one secret to cooking soups and stews on the grill: a Dutch oven. The Dutch oven allows for a slow braising of the ingredients, while the cast-iron will maintain a consistent heat and add to the flavoring; in fact, the more you use your cast-iron Dutch oven, the more flavors it will develop itself. As such, I recommend investing in a cast-iron Dutch oven from Le Creuset, Sur La Table, or any other leading brand. Farms have contributed our recipes for Beans and Escarole (page 52) as well as Creamy Parsnip Soup with Nutty Pear Salsa (page 51). Try making them once on the stovetop and once with a Dutch over and see what you prefer. I think the Dutch oven is perfect for earthy dishes made with fresh ingredients cooked over a long period of time.

CHORIZO-STUFFED MUSHROOMS

MAKES 8 TO 10 SERVINGS
ACTIVE TIME: 25 MINUTES
TOTAL TIME: 50 MINUTES

1 Spanish chorizo, casing removed

14 white mushrooms, stemmed

¼ cup plus 2 tablespoons extra-virgin olive oil

1 medium white onion, finely chopped

4 cherry tomatoes, quartered

¼ cup chicken broth

1 small bunch flat-leaf parsley, finely chopped

Coarsely ground black pepper

Fresh sea salt

These chorizo-stuffed mushrooms can be very filling, so try not to eat too many of them. The Spanish chorizo has a strong spice to it and pairs well with a glass of red wine.

1. Prepare the gas or charcoal grill to medium heat. Leave a cast-iron skillet on the grill while heating so that it develops a faint, smoky flavor.

2. While waiting, add the chorizo to a food processor and purée into a thick paste. Remove and set aside.

3. When the grill is ready, at about 350 to 400 degrees with the coals lightly covered with ash, brush the mushroom caps with 2 tablespoons of the extra-virgin olive oil. Next, place the mushroom tops on the grill and cook for about 2 minutes, until the tops have browned. Remove from the grill and place on a baking sheet.

4. Next, add the remaining ¼ cup of extra-virgin olive oil to the cast-iron skillet, followed by the onion and cherry tomatoes. Cook about 2 minutes, until the onion is translucent, and then stir in the puréed chorizo. Continue to cook about 3 minutes, until the chorizo is lightly browned, and then add the chicken broth and parsley. Cook for only a minute or so longer, and then remove from the heat.

5. Using a spoon, put the chorizo mixture into the mushroom caps. Move the baking sheet to a cool side of the grill and cook for about 15 minutes, until the chorizo has browned.

6. Remove from the grill and serve hot.

BRUSSELS SPROUT CHIPS

Courtesy of Untiedt's Vegetable Farm, Inc.
Waverly, MN

MAKES 4 TO 6 SERVINGS
ACTIVE TIME: 15 MINUTES
TOTAL TIME: 30 TO 45 MINUTES

2 cups Brussels sprouts

2 tablespoons butter, coconut oil, or any cooking oil

Coarsely ground black pepper

Fresh sea salt

Lemon zest (optional)

1. Preheat the oven to 350 degrees.

2. Peel the Brussels sprouts by trimming off the end of each sprout and peeling off the outer leaves, until you see a slightly lighter green, shiny surface emerge. You can cook just the leaves for chips or cut the remaining sprout in half and roast everything together.

3. Mix the leaves, sprouts (if using), butter, coarsely ground black pcpper, and fresh sea salt together in a bowl and add the lemon zest if desired.

4. Line two baking sheets with parchment paper and spread the mixture on them in an even layer. Bake about 10 minutes, until the leaves are crispy.

SHRIMP COCKTAIL

MAKES 10 TO 12 SERVINGS
ACTIVE TIME: 10 MINUTES
TOTAL TIME: 1 HOUR 10 MINUTES

2 pounds pre-cooked shrimp, deveined and shells removed

16 ounces organic tomato sauce

1 to 2 tablespoons fresh horseradish, depending on your preference

1 teaspoon Dijon mustard

¼ small lemon, juiced

Coarsely ground black pepper

Fresh sea salt

1 large lemon, quartered

This is a classic summer dish. Here we start with a tomato-sauce foundation, and then build upon that to arrive at a fresh and original cocktail sauce. Enjoy this chilled, perhaps with a glass of white wine.

1. Arrange the pre-cooked shrimp on a large platter and place in the refrigerator. Chill for at least 1 hour before serving.

2. In a medium bowl, mix all the remaining ingredients except the quartered lemon. Place in the refrigerator and chill for about 30 minutes.

3. Place the cocktail sauce, along with the lemon wedges, in the center of the shrimp platter. Serve chilled.

BEEFSTEAK TOMATOES WITH BASIL AND BALSAMIC VINAIGRETTE

MAKES 4 TO 6 SERVINGS
ACTIVE TIME: 10 MINUTES
TOTAL TIME: 10 MINUTES

4 beefsteak tomatoes, sliced into ½-inch pieces

½ cup fresh basil leaves

1 tablespoon extra-virgin olive oil

1 tablespoon balsamic vinegar

Coarsely ground black pepper

Fresh sea salt

I recommend serving this before the main dish, as it's not too filling and offers the perfect level of flavor before the main course.

1. Place the beefsteak tomatoes on a platter, then layer with the basil leaves.

2. In a small glass, combine the extra-virgin olive oil and balsamic vinegar, and then drizzle it evenly across the tomatoes and basil.

3. Season with the coarsely ground black pepper and fresh sea salt, and then serve immediately.

TOMATO AND TOMATILLO GAZPACHO

Courtesy of Untiedt's Vegetable Farm, Inc. Waverly, MN

½ pound fresh tomatillos, husked, rinsed, and quartered

1½ pounds tomatoes, chopped and divided

½ cup onion, chopped and divided

1 fresh Serrano chile, coarsely chopped, including seeds

1 garlic clove, quartered

2 tablespoons red wine vinegar

1¼ teaspoons salt
2 tablespoons extra-virgin olive oil

½ cup fresh cilantro, chopped

⅓ cup water (optional, for desired consistency)

1. Purée the tomatillos, half of the tomatoes, and half of the onion with the Serrano chile, garlic, red wine vinegar, and salt in a blender until smooth.

2. Force the mixture through a medium-mesh sieve into a bowl, discarding any remaining solids.

3. Stir in the remaining tomatoes and onion, water, olive oil, and cilantro. Chill until cold, at least 1 hour and up to 4 hours.

CREAMY PARSNIP SOUP WITH NUTTY PEAR SALSA

Courtesy of Chef Nancy Matsui of Onion Empire · McClendon's Select · Peoria, AZ

SERVES 8 TO 10
ACTIVE TIME: 25 MINUTES
TOTAL TIME: 40 MINUTES

FOR THE SOUP
2 tablespoons extra-virgin olive oil

2½ pounds parsnips, peeled and chopped into ½-inch to ¾-inch pieces

3 garlic cloves, minced

4 teaspoons garam masala

2 teaspoons smoked paprika

1 teaspoon cardamom

½ teaspoon kosher salt

7 cups water

2 cubes Rapunzel Vegetable Bouillon or other available bouillon, with no salt added

¾ cup half-and-half cream

¾ cup heavy cream

1 teaspoon Meyer lemon juice

FOR THE SALSA
1 D'Anjou pear diced into quarter-inch pieces

2 teaspoons Meyer lemon juice

1 tablespoon chopped flat-leaf parsley

1 tablespoon chopped fresh tarragon

¼ cup pomegranate seeds

¼ cup toasted, chopped hazelnuts

Pinch kosher salt

1. In a large saucepan, heat the extra-virgin olive oil over medium-high heat. Add the parsnips and garlic, and sauté until lightly golden.

2. Add the garam masala, paprika, cardamom, and salt, and cook 2 to 3 minutes, until fragrant. Add the water, bouillon, and both creams. Bring to a simmer and cook until the parsnips are soft.

3. Purée the soup in a blender (or use an immersion blender in the pot, but it will not be as creamy) until very smooth. Return the soup to the pot and add the lemon juice. Add ½ teaspoon of additional salt, to taste.

4. In a small bowl, combine all the salsa ingredients and mix well.

5. To serve: Ladle soup into heated bowls and top with the salsa.

BEANS AND ESCAROLE SOUP

MAKES 6 SERVINGS
ACTIVE TIME: 30 MINUTES
TOTAL TIME: 50 MINUTES

2 large heads escarole

2 stalks celery, thinly sliced

2 large cloves garlic, chopped

2 tablespoons tomato paste

Coarsely ground black pepper

Fresh sea salt

2 cups cranberry beans

Courtesy of Migliorelli Farm · Tivoli, NY

1. Wash and parboil the escarole, saving 4 cups of water (discard the rest). Chop the escarole.

2. Add the celery, garlic, tomato paste, and coarsely ground black pepper and fresh sea salt to the escarole water. Cook over low-medium heat for 20 minutes.

3. Add the beans and cook until almost tender. Add the chopped escarole and cook until tender.

TIP: SERVE WITH WARM BREAD AND RED PEPPER FLAKES.

CLASSIC CAESAR SALAD

MAKES 6 SERVINGS
ACTIVE TIME: 15 MINUTES
TOTAL TIME: 30 MINUTES

3 heads Romaine lettuce

2 garlic cloves, minced

½ small lemon, juiced

1 large egg

4 anchovy filets

1 teaspoon Dijon mustard

½ cup extra-virgin olive oil

Coarsely ground black pepper

Fresh sea salt

Fresh Parmesan (optional)

Croutons (optional)

Anchovy filets are an essential ingredient to the Classic Caesar Salad.

1. Rinse the heads of the Romaine lettuce and then dry thoroughly. Place in the refrigerator.

2. In a small bowl, whisk the garlic, lemon juice, and egg until blended. Whisk in the anchovy filets and Dijon mustard, until the anchovies have been completely incorporated into the dressing.

3. Gradually whisk in the extra-virgin olive oil and then season with the coarsely ground black pepper and sea salt. Place the dressing in the refrigerator for about 15 minutes and then pour over the chilled Romaine lettuce. Serve immediately, with fresh shaved Parmesan.

TIP: FOR HOMEMADE CROUTONS, BREAK APART COUNTRY SOURDOUGH (PAGE 207) INTO HALF-INCH PIECES AND PLACE THEM ON A BAKING SHEET. TOAST FOR ABOUT 15 MINUTES AT 350 DEGREES SO THAT THE PIECES HARDEN, MAKING THE PERFECT CRUNCH IN YOUR SALAD.

HOUSE SALAD

MAKES 6 SERVINGS
ACTIVE TIME: 15 MINUTES
TOTAL TIME: 30 MINUTES

3 heads Romaine lettuce

1 small red onion, sliced into ¼-inch rings

10 Kalamata olives

10 green olives

4 plum tomatoes, stemmed and quartered

6 pepperoncini peppers

2 garlic cloves, minced

¼ cup red wine vinegar

¾ cup extra-virgin olive oil

Coarsely ground black pepper

Fresh sea salt

This basic, hearty salad is a good complement to prime rib.

1. Rinse the heads of the lettuce and dry them thoroughly. In a medium bowl, combine the lettuce, red onion, Kalamata olives, green olives, tomatoes, and pepperoncini peppers and set in the refrigerator.

2. In a small jar, whisk together the garlic, red wine vinegar, and extra-virgin olive oil, and then season with the coarsely ground black pepper and fresh sea salt. Chill in the refrigerator for 15 minutes.

3. Remove the salad and vinaigrette from the refrigerator and mix together. Serve immediately.

ARUGULA SALAD WITH TARRAGON-SHALLOT VINAIGRETTE

MAKES 6 SERVINGS
ACTIVE TIME: 10 MINUTES
TOTAL TIME: 10 MINUTES

1 pound Arugula, stemmed

1 shallot, minced

5 stalks tarragon, minced

¼ small lemon, juiced

1 teaspoon Dijon mustard

½ cup extra-virgin olive oil

3 tablespoons red wine vinegar

Coarsely ground black pepper

Fresh sea salt

This hearty salad is quick to make and full of flavor. Serve it with white wine.

1. Rinse the arugula and then dry thoroughly. Place in the refrigerator and set aside.

2. In a small bowl, whisk together the shallot, tarragon, lemon juice, and Dijon mustard, and then slowly add in the extra-virgin olive oil and red wine vinegar.

3. Season with the coarsely ground black pepper and fresh sea salt, and then pour over the arugula. Serve immediately.

RADICCHIO SALAD WITH BOK CHOY

Courtesy of Muth Family Farm Williamstown, NJ

MAKES 6 SERVINGS
ACTIVE TIME: 20 MINUTES
TOTAL TIME: 45 MINUTES

2 tablespoons apple cider vinegar

1 tablespoon Dijon mustard

1 tablespoon honey or agave

¼ cup extra-virgin olive oil

Coarsely ground black pepper

Fresh sea salt

1 medium to large head radicchio, finely chopped into thin ribbons

2 cups chopped bok choy (leaves and stalks)

1 cup chopped romaine lettuce

1 apple, chopped

1 cup chopped walnuts, toasted

½ cup dried cranberries

⅓ cup crumbled gorgonzola cheese (optional)

1. In a small bowl, combine the apple cider vinegar, Dijon mustard, honey, extra-virgin olive oil, coarsely ground black pepper, and fresh sea salt, and whisk to blend. Set aside.

2. In a large bowl, combine the rest of the ingredients. Add the dressing and toss.

CELERIAC AND MACHE RIBBON SALAD

MAKES 4 SERVINGS
ACTIVE TIME: 15 MINUTES
**TOTAL TIME: 1 HOUR AND
15 MINUTES**

1 to 2 heads celery root
(1 pound)

1 tablespoon Dijon
mustard

2 tablespoons apple
cider

4 tablespoons extra-
virgin olive oil

2 teaspoons lemon juice

Coarsely ground black
pepper

Fresh sea salt

4 cups mache or
watercress leaves

2 tablespoons
toasted walnuts,
chopped coarsely

Courtesy of Glynwood · Cold Spring, NY

1. Peel the tough, outer layer of the celery root and slice the ends off. Continue to peel until all the rough edges are gone. Cut the celery root head into 6 to 8 pieces (cut head in half, then each half into three sections and square off each piece, approximately 1 inch wide).

2. Using a vegetable peeler with a wide blade, peel "ribbons" off the celery root sections. Continue with each piece of root until it's all peeled (you might have smaller pieces left that you could not peel).

3. Blend the mustard, cider, olive oil, and lemon juice in a food processor or blender. Season with the coarsely ground black pepper and fresh sea salt. Combine the dressing with the celery root ribbons, coating all pieces. Let the salad rest for 1 hour. Toss the mache or watercress leaves into the salad. Sprinkle the walnut pieces over the salad.

WHEAT BERRY SALAD

Courtesy of Muth Family Farm
Williamstown, NJ

MAKES 6 SERVINGS
ACTIVE TIME: 30 MINUTES
TOTAL TIME: 1 HOUR AND
15 MINUTES

1½ cups wheat berries
(such as Einkorn)

2½ cups water

½ teaspoon salt

1 large bunch kale, ribs
removed, cut into thin
ribbons

3 tablespoons extra-
virgin olive oil

¾ cups walnuts or
pecans, chopped and
toasted

1 cup chopped
cucumbers (remove
skins if they're tough)

1 tablespoon chopped
chives

½ cup dried
cranberries

½ cup fresh parsley,
finely chopped (large
stems removed and
discarded)

2 tablespoons freshly
squeezed lemon juice

Coarsely ground black
pepper

Fresh sea salt

1. Put the wheat berries in a large pot, and cover with the water. Add the salt and bring to a boil. Reduce heat, and simmer for 50 to 60 minutes, covered, until tender. Drain and set aside to cool.

2. Meanwhile, sauté the kale in 1 tablespoon of the extra-virgin olive oil, until it reaches desired tenderness. Set aside to cool.

3. In a large bowl, combine the wheat berries, kale, nuts, cucumbers, chives, cranberries, parsley, the remaining extra-virgin olive oil, and the lemon juice. Season to taste with the coarsely ground black pepper and fresh sea salt.

BEEF-WORTHY BEER AND WINE

PERFECT PAIRINGS

By Carlo DeVito

Kevin Zraly, the author of *Windows on the World Wine Course*, has said that we are living in the golden age of wine. Never before has so much wine been produced, in so many places, and at the same time. Consumption of wine is at an all-time high.

You could say the same thing of beer. The craft beer world—the second generation, so to speak, after the original boom of the '90s—has exploded like almost nothing else. There are microbreweries, farm-to-table breweries, collaboration beers, and new styles popping up every day.

When biting into a juicy piece of steak, whether you like it rare, medium, or well done, whether you like a nice, juicy center-cut, or a roasty end, having a glass of wine or craft beer to accentuate the chewy morsel is what the experience is all about.

Of course, we've got a list of classic reds from around the world. We've taken care to represent the classic regions such as France, Italy, and Spain, as well as new world regions like Australia, South Africa, and South America: big, hearty wines, with power, finesse, and complexity made from a range of varieties.

We've also taken care to shake things up a little. Wine is now made in all fifty states. And there are a lot of good ones being made all around the country. Many meals today are made using local ingredients, so we've made sure to include not only some classic wines from California, Oregon, and Washington but also wines from across the country like New York, Virginia, Maryland, Colorado, and Texas, to name a few. And of course, we've included the new and fabulous wines of Canada from regions like the Niagara Bench, Ontario, and Okanagan Valley. All these wines are tremendous elixirs, capable of competing in world markets, and worthy of being searched out.

Steak and a beer are a classic pairing. As with wine, beer has made huge strides. Today, beer has more going for it than almost any other category. Yes, mass producers still dominate the market, but there is more variety these days in terms of producers and styles than ever before. And yes, a pilsner can perform amiably well. But, the new understanding of beer and the connoisseurship of beer are much more in the spotlight. Now, the best restaurants are cellaring not only wines but beers as well, and a cellar master is engaged at the best places. Brown ales, dubbels, ESBs, porters, and stouts have all grown in style and substance to provide the perfect complement to the juicy piece of steak at the end of your fork. We've taken care to find some of the best from around the world.

Whether your preference is for wine or beer, the following pages hold more than 200 suggestions to help accompany your meal and offer up some exciting options to friends and family for their perfect Prime experience.

50 BEST BEERS FOR BEEF

By Joshua M. Bernstein, author
of *The Complete Beer Course*

Properly made prime rib is a work of carnivorous art, with a dark brown crust, white swirls of creamy fat, and a juicy center, by turns pink and tender. Such well-calibrated culinary precision demands the ideal accompanying beverage, for which I look toward beer. Overly bitter IPAs are banished from this feast, as are light lagers and smooth-sipping wheat beers. Instead, I opt for beers boasting maltier profiles and a bit more heft, such as stouts or porters. The roasty characteristics will complement the crackling exterior, while the bitterness will help contrast the meat's opulence. For a different road, an ESB's caramel-focused flavor makes it a fine companion to prime rib, as is a rich and malty Belgian-style dubbel. Lastly, one of the most beef-friendly beer styles is the nutty, toffee-noted brown ale. (American versions feature a more pronounced hop profile.) Here are fifty fantastic beers to sip alongside your next slice of prime rib.

BROWN ALE

Big Sky Moose Drool

Brooklyn Brewery Brown Ale

Dogfish Head Indian Brown Ale

Parallel 49 Old Boy Ale

Pretty Things Beer and Ale Project Saint Botolph's Town

Rogue Hazelnut Brown Nectar

Samuel Smith's Nut Brown Ale

Smuttynose Old Brown Dog

Surly Bender

Upslope Brown Ale

DUBBEL

Allagash Dubbel Ale

Belgh Brasse Mons Abbey Dubbel

Chimay Première

Goose Island Père Jacques

Microbrasserie Charlevoix Dominus Vobiscum Double

New Belgium Abbey

Ommegang Abbey Ale

St. Bernardus Prior 8

Trappistes Rochefort 6

Westmalle Trappist Dubbel

ESB

AleSmith Anvil Ale ESB

Central City Red Racer ESB

Grand Teton Bitch Creek ESB

Left Hand Sawtooth Ale

Redhook ESB

Schlafly ESB

Stoudt's Scarlet Lady ESB

Wells Bombardier

Yards Extra Special Ale

Young's Special London Ale

PORTER

Alaskan Smoked Porter

Anchor Porter

Fuller's London Porter

Great Lakes Edmund Fitzgerald Porter

Founders Porter

Harviestoun Old Engine Oil

Meantime London Porter

Russell Black Death Porter

Stone Smoked Porter

Tröegs Dead Reckoning Porter

STOUT

Avery Out of Bounds Stout

Bar Harbor Cadillac Mountain Stout

Bell's Kalamazoo Stout

Deschutes Obsidian Stout

Dieu Du Ciel Aphrodisiaque

Magic Hat Heart of Darkness

Modern Times Black House

North Coast Old No. 38 Stout

Porterhouse Wrasslers XXXX Stout

Sierra Nevada Stout

WINES FOR PRIME DINNERS: UNITED STATES WINE LIST

By Dave McIntyre, wine columnist for *The Washington Post*

Prime rib has an atavistic, cave-man appeal, a Flintstonian piece of meat that deserves a wine equally primal and masculine. Cabernet Sauvignon and its friends Merlot, Cabernet Franc, and Malbec come to mind—and certainly, any Bordeaux would do, especially a first or second growth. And Bordeaux has its disciples around the world, including Cabernets from Napa Valley and Washington State, and the newly emerging Bordeaux-styled wines from the Eastern United States. Any of these would dance well with prime rib.

"There is no one right answer when it comes to pairing wine with a great piece of beef," says Master Sommelier Carlton J. McCoy, Jr., wine director at the Little Nell in Aspen, Colorado. "Essentially, the wine must have the requisite amount of both tannin and acid to balance the rich marbling of the meat."

Prime rib gives young wines a chance to strut their stuff—"fat cuts tannin," after all. Yet it also allows a well-aged wine to shine, like soft light illuminating a museum masterpiece. Season and sauce it simply, and prime rib becomes a suitable showcase for that special wine in your cellar—you know, the one you've been holding for a special occasion that never seems to come. McCoy favors those older reds, ones that have settled down and no longer need to show off. But as he says, there's no one right answer. The possibilities are endless.

Here are my personal recommendations:

Carlton McCoy's Domestic Recommendations

1987 Diamond Creek Gravelly Meadow

1984 Ridge Montebello

NAPA VALLEY

Robert Mondavi Reserve Cabernet Sauvignon, Oakville

Stag's Leap Wine Cellars, S.L.V. Cabernet Sauvignon, Stag's Leap District

Diamond Creek Gravelly Meadow Cabernet Sauvignon

Smith-Madrone Cabernet Sauvignon

Cakebread Cellars Cabernet Sauvignon

Saddleback Cellars

Cabernet Sauvignon

Beckstoffer To Kalon Vineyard Cabernet Sauvignon

Joseph Phelps Insignia

Oberon Cabernet Sauvignon

Frog's Leap Cabernet Sauvignon

Ironstone Vineyards Cabernet Franc

Charles Krug Generations

Antica Cabernet Sauvignon

Chateau Montelena Cabernet Sauvignon

Heritance Cabernet Sauvignon

SONOMA COUNTY

Gundlach-Bundschu Vintage Reserve, Sonoma Valley

Dry Creek Vineyard The Mariner, Dry Creek Valley

Littorai Hirsch Vineyard Pinot Noir, Sonoma Coast

Ramey Wine Cellars Cole Creek Vineyard

Syrah, Russian River Valley

Bedrock Wine Co. The Bedrock Heritage, Sonoma Valley

Mauritson Rockpile Zinfandel, Rockpile

Arnot-Roberts Clary Ranch Syrah, Sonoma Coast

Pedroncelli Zinfandel Mother Clone, Dry Creek Valley

Cameron Hughes Lot 230 Cabernet Sauvignon, Chalk Hill

Alexander Valley Vineyards Temptation Zinfandel, Alexander Valley

OTHER CALIFORNIA

Ridge Monte Bello Cabernet Sauvignon, Santa Cruz Mountains

Stolpman The Originals Syrah, Ballard Canyon, Santa Barbara County

Qupé Bien Nacido Vineyard Syrah, Santa Maria Valley, Santa Barbara County

Sandhi Pinot Noir, Santa Rita Hills, Santa Barbara County

Daou Reserve Cabernet

Sauvignon, Paso Robles

Zin-Phomaniac Old Vines Zinfandel, Lodi

Calder Wine Company Carignane, Mendocino County

PACIFIC NORTHWEST

Domaine Drouhin Pinot Noir, Dundee Hills, Willamette Valley, Oregon

The Eyrie Vineyards Pinot Noir, Willamette Valley, Oregon

Andrew Will Two Blondes Vineyard, Yakima Valley, Washington

Chateau Ste. Michelle Cabernet Sauvignon, Canoe Ridge Estate, Columbia Valley, Washington

Leonetti Cellar Merlot, Walla Walla Valley, Washington

L'Ecole No. 41 Perigee, Seven Hills Vineyard, Walla Walla Valley, Washington

Long Shadows Vintners Sequel Syrah, Columbia Valley, Washington

Quilceda Creek Cabernet Sauvignon, Columbia Valley, Washington

Browne Family Tribute

Red Blend, Columbia Valley, Washington

OTHER UNITED STATES

Markko Vineyard Cabernet Sauvignon, Conneaut, Ohio

RdV Vineyards Lost Mountain, Delaplane, Virginia

Barboursville Vineyards Octagon, Barboursville, Virginia

Bedell Cellars Merlot, North Fork of Long Island, New York

King Family Vineyards Meritage, Monticello, Virginia

Boordy Vineyards Landmark Reserve, Hydes, Maryland

Stinson Vineyards Tannat, Crozet, Virginia

Black Ankle Vineyards Crumbling Rock, Mt. Airy, Maryland

Veritas Vineyard and Winery Petit Verdot, Monticello, Virginia

Stone Hill Winery Cross J Vineyard Norton, Hermann, Missouri

Glen Manor Vineyards, Hodder Hill, Front Royal, Virginia

Linden Vineyards Hardscrabble, Linden, Virginia

Boxwood Winery Topiary, Middleburg, Virginia

Pedernales Cellars, Texas Tempranillo, Stonewall, Texas

Brennan Vineyards Tempranillo, Comanche, Texas

McPherson Cellars Les Copains, Lubbock, Texas

Sawtooth Winery Skyline Red, Nampa, Idaho

Ruby Trust Cellars The Smuggler, Castle Rock, Colorado

The Infinite Monkey Theorem 100th Monkey, Denver, Colorado

Shinn Estate Vineyards Merlot, North Fork of Long Island, New York

Shady Lane Cellars Blue Franc, Leelanau Peninsula, Michigan

Breaux Vineyards Nebbiolo, Purcelville, Virginia

Caduceus Cellars Anubis, Jerome, Arizona

Allegro Winery and Vineyards Cadenza, Brogue, Pennsylvania

CANADIAN REDS, READY FOR PRIME RIB

By Rémy Charest, wine writer and judge based in Québec City

In Canada, Alberta is where the top beef comes from, but the wines that go with the top cuts are mostly grown in Ontario and British Columbia, where the bulk of Canadian wine production takes place. Generally speaking, Pinot noir and Cabernet Franc have been the standout red grapes (along with Chardonnay and Riesling on the white front), but in recent years, Syrah has been garnering high scores and high praise in national competitions like the National Wine Awards of Canada, thanks to a cool-climate feeling that can surely please lovers of Northern Rhône wines. Making big, Cabernet Sauvignon–based Bordeaux blends can be a bit more challenging in cooler years, but top estates in Ontario and British Columbia get it right in their top cuvées. It's a young industry, still open to experimenting and trying new stuff, as you can see, with cuvées integrating Malbec, Touriga Nacional, or even delicious reds from hybrid grapes produced in cooler areas like Québec, where one biodynamic estate, Les Pervenches, has been leading the way. And even though it might be a touch on the light side for prime rib, you really should try some of Ontario's best Pinot, especially from the up-and-coming, limestone-rich terroir of Prince Edward County.

BRITISH COLUMBIA

Laughing Stock Vineyards Syrah, Perfect Hedge Vineyard

Mission Hill Compendium

Moon Curser Vineyards Touriga Nacional

Nk'Mip Cellars Qwam Qwmt Cabernet Sauvignon

Osoyoos Larose Le Grand Vin

Road 13 Vineyards Syrah Malbec

Stag's Hollow Syrah

ONTARIO

Château des Charmes Equuleus, Paul Bosc Estate Vineyard

Creekside Estate

Winery Broken Press Syrah, Queenston Road Vineyard

Flat Rock Cellars Pinot Noir

Hidden Bench Terroir Caché

Norman Hardie Winery and Vineyard County Pinot Noir

Southbrook Vineyards Triomphe Cabernet Franc

Tawse Winery Cabernet Franc, Laundry Vineyard

Vineland Estates Winery Cabernet Franc

QUEBEC

Vignoble Les Pervenches Cuvée de Montmollin (Maréchal Foch)

WORLDLY WINES

By Howard G. Goldberg, editor of
The New York Times Book of Wine

Instead of sending a turkey "twice the size of Tiny Tim" to Camden Town by horse-drawn cab, if the reformed Ebenezer Scrooge had taken the Cratchits to chandelier-lit Simpson's-in-the-Strand surely Christmas dinner would have been a thick prime rib roast carved tableside on an antique silver-domed butler's dolly by a chef wearing a white toque and white apron. (Assuming that "upon Christmas Day," as Bob Cratchit might have said, the restaurant was indeed open.)

Simpson's, founded in 1828, was a favorite of Charles Dickens. And Claret—red wine from Bordeaux—was synonymous (as were after-dinner cigars and port) with gentlemen's dining in London's oak-paneled rooms in Victorian times.

Although Simpson's future was in doubt in early 2015, more than 171 years after *A Christmas Carol* was published, tradition still clung tightly: Bordeaux reds led its shortened wine list posted online. British Francophilia was expressed in the descending tiers of the hierarchy: Burgundy, Beaujolais, Rhône—and then (a mite dismissively?) "rest of the world."

The list's sole representative from Argentina was, aptly, a Malbec. In that beef-crazed country, the two it takes to tango are Malbec, the country's strong red suit, and roast prime rib, which is called *asado* (the same word that denotes cooking meat on a grill).

All sorts of reds produced outside the United States and Canada can pair winningly with prime rib. You can fill your glass from France, Italy, Spain, Argentina, Chile, South Africa, Australia, New Zealand, Greece, Lebanon, Austria, Portugal, Germany, or Portugal.

Because ideal slabs of edge-to-edge pink, browned, salt-crusted, funky, bone-in (or out) rib roast are richly marbled, robust, juicy, tender, smooth, and fine-grained, when they are onstage—on the dinner table—they are scripted to play the meal's leading role. The beef's accompanying reds should not challenge its primacy but, Oscar-like, function as best supporting actor (or actress, if you prefer)

Since vintages vary in quality, consumers should first do their homework in selecting bottles. They can make their search relatively easy by focusing on high-standard, top-quality producers who year in and year out dependably strive to make the best of what mercurial Mother Nature deals out. (They need not waste time on the metaphysical issue of whether any white wine can wash down the beef.)

The accompanying alphabetical listing of red wine producers can serve as a buying guide. Though citations of proprietary names on labels tend to signify blends, some wines may stem from a lone grape variety.

FRANCE

Bernard Baudry (Loire); Chinon cabernet franc

Château Chasse-Spleen (Bordeaux); Moulis-en-Médoc

Château de Beaucastel (Rhône); Châteauneuf-du-Pape

Château Lagrézette (Cahors); Le Pigeonnier label

Château Phélan Ségur (Bordeaux); Saint-Estèphe

Château Sociando-Mallet (Bordeaux); Haut-Médoc

Domaine Comte Abbatucci (Corsica); Rouge Frais Impérial

Domaine de Chevalier (Pessac-Léognan, Bordeaux); Graves

Domaine du Clos du Fief, Michel Tête (Beaujolais); Juliénas

Domaine du Vieux Télégraphe (Rhône); Châteauneuf-du-Pape

Domaine Léon Barra (Languedoc-Roussillon); Faugères

Domaine Tempier (Bandol, Provence); Cabassaou, La Migoua and La Tourtine labels

E. Guigal; Rhône appellations

Éric Texier; Rhône locales

J. L. Chave; Rhône appellations

Joseph Drouhin; Burgundy appellations

Louis Jadot; Burgundy appellations

Marcel Lapierre (Beaujolais); Morgon

Olga Raffault (Chinon); Les Picasses

Paul Jaboulet Aîné; various Rhônes

ITALY

Alois Legeder (Alto Adige); a Lagrein and also the Römigberg Kalterersee Classico, made from Schiava

Arianna Occhipinti (Sicily); SP68 Frapatto e Nero d'Avola, a blend

Avignonesi (Tuscany); Vino Nobile di Montepulciano, Rosso di Montepulciano

Badia a Coltibuono (Tuscany); Chianti Classico

Capezzana (Tuscany); Villa di Capezzana Carmignano and Trefiano Riserva Carmignano labels

Castello Banfi (Tuscany); Brunello di Montalcino, Rosso di Montalcino

Castello di Nipozzano—Marchesi de' Frescobaldi (Tuscany); a broad palette of labels

Elio Grasso (Langhe, Piedmont); Barolo, Barbera d'Alba, a Nebbiolo

Elisabetta Foradori (Alto Adige); Teroldego

Fontodi (Tuscany); Chianti Classico

J. Hofstätter (Alto Adige); Pinot Nero

Le Macchiole (Bolgheri, Tuscany); Super-Tuscans

Marchesi Antinori (Tuscany); a wide variety of bottlings

Marchesi di Barolo (Langhe, Piedmont); Barolo, Barbaresco, Barbera

Mastroberardino (Campania); Taurasi Radici Reserva

Paolo Scavino (Piedmont); Barolo, Barbera, Dolcetto d'Alba and a Nebbiolo

Planeta (Sicily); Nero d'Avola

Produttori del Barbaresco (Piedmont); a cooperative specializing in Barbaresco

Renato Ratti (Langhe, Piedmont); Barolo

Vietti (Piedmont); Tre Vigne Barbera d'Asti and Tre Vigne Barbera d'Alba

SPAIN

Alvar Palacios (Priorat); Camins del Priorat label

Celler de Capçanes Peraj Ha'abib (Montsant, Spain); kosher

Clos Mogador (Priorat); Manyetes label

Compañía de Vinos Telmo Rodríguez (Rioja); Altos de Lanzaga

Condado de Haza (Ribera del Duero); Alenza Gran Reserva, Condado de Haza labels

CVNE, Compañía Vinicola del Norte de España (Rioja); Imperial Gran Reserva

Jiménez-Landi (Méntrida); The End, a Garnacha

Marqués de Murrieta (Rioja); Castillo Ygay Gran Reserva Especial

Marqués de Riscal (Rioja); Gran Reserva

Miguel Torres (Penedès); multiple sourcings

Muga (Rioja); Torre Muga

Numanthia (Toro); Termanthia label

Protos (Ribera del Duero); Selección Finca el Grajo Viej

R. López de Heredia (Rioja); Viña Tondonia Red Reserva

Viña Ardanza (Rioja); Reserva

ARGENTINA

Catena Zapata (Mendoza); Malbec, Cabernet Sauvignon

Colomé (Salta); Malbec

Dominio del Plata (Mendoza); Crios, Benmarco, Susana Balbo (the winemaker) and Nosotros labels

Familia Zuccardi (Mendoza); Bonarda, Cabernet Sauvignon, Malbec

Salentein (Mendoza); Malbec

Terrazas de los Andes (Mendoza); Los Compuertas (Malbec) and Los Aromos (Cabernet Sauvignon) labels

CHILE

Casa Lapostolle; Cuvée Alexandre, Apalta Vineyard (Colchagua Valley)

Concha y Toro; Carmín de Peumo Carménère (Cachapoal Valley)

Errázuriz; Don Maximiano Founder's Reserve (Aconcagua Valley)

Montes; Alpha Cabernet Sauvignon, Alpha Carménère, Alpha Malbec (Colchagua Valley)

SOUTH AFRICA

Crystallum (Swartland); Cuvée Peter Max Pinot Noir

Hamilton Russell Vineyards (Hemel-en-Aarde Valley); Pinot Noir

Kanonkop (Stellenbosch); Pinotage, Paul Sauer label

Meerlust (Stellenbosch); Cabernet Sauvignon, Merlot and the Rubicon label

Mullineux Family Wines (Swartland); Syrah

Reyneke (Stellenbosch); Syrah and the Reserve Red label

Rustenberg (Stellenbosch); Peter Barlow Cabernet Sauvignon and John X Merriman (blend) labels

Vergelegen (Stellenbosch); Reserve Cabernet Sauvignon, Mill Race Merlot, Vergelegen V label

Warwick (Stellenbosch); Cabernet Franc and the Trilogy label

Waterkloof (Stellenbosch); Circumstance Syrah and the Circle of Life Red label

AUSTRALIA

Clarendon Hills (McLaren Vale); Domaine Clarendon, a Syrah; Cabernet Sauvignons, Grenaches, Syrahs

Cullen (Margaret River); Diana Madeline label

d'Arenberg (McLaren Vale); The Dead Arm Shiraz

Giant Steps (Yarra Valley); Sexton Vineyard Pinot Noir

Jacob's Creek (Barossa Valley); Reserve Shiraz

Mac Forbes (Yarra Valley); Pinot Noir

Moss Wood (Margaret River); Cabernet Sauvignon

Penfolds (Adelaide); Shiraz, Cabernet Sauvignon

Wolf Blass (Barossa Valley); Shiraz, Cabernet Sauvignon

Yarra Yering (Yarra Valley); Dry Red No. 1 and Dry Red No. 2

NEW ZEALAND

Ata Rangi (Martinborough); Pinot Noir

Craggy Range (Martinborough); Te Muna Road Vineyard Pinot Noir, Gimblett Gravels Vineyard Merlot

Felton Road (Central Otago); Pinot Noir

Kevin Judd Greywacke (Marlborough); Pinot Noir

Rippon (Central Otago); Mature Vine Pinot Noir

OTHER COUNTRIES

Alpha Estate (Amyndeon, Greece); Xinomavro

Boutari (Greece); Grande Reserve Naoussa, a Xinomavro

Chateau Musar (Lebanon); Bordeaux-style blend

Domaine du Castel (Israel); Grand Vin Haute Judée, Bordeaux-style blend

Niepoort (Portugal); Douro Batuta, Charme labels

Paul Achs (Burgenland, Austria); Blaufränkisch (Lemberger)

Recanati (Israel); Cabernet Sauvignon

Rudolf Fürst (Franconia, Germany); Spätburgunder (Pinot Noir)

Umathum (Burgenland, Austria); Blaufränkisch (Lemberger), Saint Laurent, Zweigelt

Wine & Soul (Douro, Portugal); Pintas Character label

RUBS & MARINADES
(ELEMENTS OF STYLE)

SOUTHWESTERN DRY RUB

1 small garlic clove, diced

2 teaspoons fresh thyme, minced

2 tablespoons dry mustard

1 tablespoon onion powder

1 teaspoon ground coriander

1 teaspoon celery powder

¼ cup kosher salt

1 tablespoon coarsely ground black pepper

1 tablespoon coarsely ground white pepper

1 tablespoon extra-virgin olive oil

Perfect for a grilled, prime rib dinner in the summer, be sure to apply this rub to the rib roast sooner rather than later, allowing the flavors to properly seep into the meat's marbled edges. If you feel like it, maybe even put some presoaked hickory woodchips on the coals to add even more flavors to the roast.

1. Using a spoon, combine all the ingredients except the extra-virgin olive oil in a small bowl and mix thoroughly.

2. Slowly mix in the extra-virgin olive oil, and then let the rub stand at room temperature for about 30 minutes before applying to the rib roast.

VARIATION: IF YOU'D LIKE A BIT MORE OF A KICK, ADD A SEEDED AND FINELY CHOPPED HABANERO PEPPER TO THE INGREDIENTS.

TIP: BEFORE TRANSFERRING THE RIB ROAST TO THE OVEN, LET IT STAND AT ROOM TEMPERATURE FOR ABOUT 30 MINUTES SO IT CAN PROPERLY ABSORB THE RUB'S FLAVORS.

HERBAL RUB

¼ cup flat-leaf parsley, finely chopped

¼ cup fresh rosemary, finely chopped

4 to 6 medium garlic cloves, diced

1 tablespoon coarsely ground black pepper

2 tablespoons fresh sea salt

¼ cup extra-virgin olive oil

When I think of the picturesque prime rib, I always come back to a slow-roasted rib roast on Christmas morning with rosemary and thyme tied between the ribs. This rub takes those flavors and gets them ingrained into the meat. Be sure to add extra seasoning all around the ends.

1. In a small bowl, thoroughly combine the parsley, rosemary, garlic, black pepper, and sea salt.

2. Next, slowly whisk in the extra-virgin olive oil, until the ingredients form a smooth paste.

3. Let the rub stand at room temperature for 30 minutes before applying to the rib roast.

4. Let the roast marinate for 1 hour.

VARIATION: IF YOU'D LIKE TO TURN THE RUB INTO A MARINADE, INCREASE THE AMOUNT OF EXTRA-VIRGIN OLIVE OIL TO 1½ CUPS. TRANSFER THE MARINADE INTO A LARGE BOWL, FOLLOWED BY THE RIB ROAST. NOTE THAT THE RIB ROAST WILL NOT BE FULLY SUBMERGED IN THE MARINADE, SO BE SURE TO ROTATE IT THROUGHOUT THE MARINATING PROCESS IN ORDER FOR ALL SIDES OF THE ROAST TO RECEIVE EQUAL MARINATING TIME.

ANCHO CHILE RUB

2 tablespoons extra-virgin olive oil

3 tablespoons dried ancho chile powder

4 medium garlic cloves, diced

2 teaspoons ground cinnamon

2 teaspoons dried oregano

2 teaspoons unsweetened cocoa powder

2 tablespoons coarsely ground black pepper

1½ tablespoons fresh sea salt

Unlike regular chile powder, ancho chile powder comes from the ancho chile pepper, which is actually fairly sweet and works perfectly when applied mildly to the rib roast. When using this rub, always have a glass of red wine on the ready!

In a small bowl, mix together all the ingredients and let stand at room temperature for 30 minutes before applying to the rib roast.

GARLIC & CHIVE RUB

⅓ cup, plus 2 teaspoons extra-virgin olive oil

1 tablespoon fresh sea salt

6 garlic cloves, diced

4 scallions, finely chopped

¼ cup chives, coarsely chopped

1 tablespoon coarsely ground black pepper

Chives and garlic are the perfect match when rubbed onto prime rib. When roasted, the naturally strong flavors in both the chives and garlic are lightened and should always be served with a Classic Baked Potato (page 162).

1. Add 2 teaspoons of the extra-virgin olive oil to a small sauté pan. Place over low heat and then add the salt.

2. When the oil is hot and the sea salt is sizzling in the pan, add the garlic and scallions and sauté until the garlic is golden and the scallions are slightly translucent. Transfer the mixture to a small bowl and stir in the chives.

3. Gradually whisk in the remaining extra-virgin olive oil, and then season with the coarsely ground black pepper. Let the rub stand for 30 minutes before applying to the rib roast.

HORSERADISH CRUST

½ cup (1 stick) unsalted butter, softened

6 garlic cloves

¾ cup freshly grated horseradish

¼ cup fresh thyme, finely chopped

2 tablespoons fresh rosemary, minced

3 tablespoons coarsely ground black pepper

2 tablespoons fresh sea salt

This sharp horseradish crust goes hand in hand with the classic rib roast and its mild flavors. Before transferring the rib roast to the oven, the horseradish crust should be generously applied on all sides of the meat so that the flavors of the horseradish and herbs seep into the marbled edges of the rib roast.

1. In a small food processor, pulse together the softened butter, garlic, and horseradish. Transfer to a medium bowl.

2. Mash the remaining ingredients into the bowl and then let stand at room temperature for 30 minutes before applying to the rib roast.

VARIATION: IF YOU'D LIKE TO USE AN OIL-BASED CRUST, SUBSTITUTE THE BUTTER WITH ¾ CUP EXTRA-VIRGIN OLIVE OIL. THERE'S NOW NO NEED FOR A FOOD PROCESSOR, SO YOU CAN COMBINE ALL THE INGREDIENTS IN A MEDIUM BOWL.

TIP: WHEN YOU APPLY THE HORSERADISH PASTE TO THE RIB ROAST, TAKE EXTRA TIME MASSAGING THE PASTE INTO THE MEAT SO THAT ITS FLAVOR IS FULLY ABSORBED INTO THE MARBLED SECTION OF THE ROAST.

LAVENDER RUB

3 tablespoons extra-virgin olive oil

2 tablespoons dried lavender, minced

2 teaspoons fresh thyme, finely chopped

1 teaspoon fresh rosemary, finely chopped

2 tablespoons fresh sea salt

1 tablespoon coarsely ground black pepper

Although both the scent and taste of lavender are subtle, when used on prime rib it can be very powerful if applied generously. The recipe that follows features a small proportion of lavender. It will not cover the entire rib roast, so be sure to apply lightly to the meat side of the rib roast.

In a small bowl, mash all the ingredients into a paste and let stand at room temperature for 30 minutes before applying to the meat side of the rib roast.

RUSTIC PEPPER DRY RUB

2 garlic cloves, minced

2 teaspoons fresh thyme, finely chopped

2 teaspoons fresh sea salt

1½ teaspoons coarsely ground black pepper

1½ teaspoons coarsely ground white pepper

1 teaspoon coarsely ground red pepper

1 teaspoon sweet paprika

½ teaspoon onion powder

A little spicy, I recommend using this rub on a summer evening when you decide to cook the roast with either the One-Pot (page 112) or Charcoal Pit (page 100) techniques. Serve with some Baked Asparagus (page 171).

In a small bowl, stir together all the ingredients and then apply generously to the rib roast, massaging the rub into the marbled section of the roast so that the spices become properly ingrained in the meat.

DILL & CORIANDER RUB

3 tablespoons coarsely ground black pepper

3 tablespoons coriander seeds

2 tablespoons fresh dill, minced

2 medium garlic cloves, minced

2 tablespoons fresh sea salt

The sweet, natural flavors found in dill and coriander seeds are perfect when scattered on top of the rib roast. Be sure not too apply too much of this rub to the roast because the rub tends to have much more flavor than you'd expect.

In a medium bowl, combine all the ingredients and whisk together thoroughly. Allow the rib roast to rest at room temperature for 1 hour before seasoning with the rub.

VARIATION: THE DILL & CORIANDER RUB ALSO WORKS WELL AS A BASTING MARINADE. TO DO SO, ADD 1 CUP OF EXTRA-VIRGIN OLIVE OIL TO THE INGREDIENTS IN THE MEDIUM BOWL. FOLLOW MOM'S PERFECT PRIME RIB RECIPE ON PAGE 93, BASTING WITH THE DILL & CORIANDER MARINADE EVERY 20 MINUTES UNTIL FINISHED.

LEMON-SALT RUB

3 tablespoons lemon zest

3 tablespoons fresh sea salt

1 tablespoon coarsely ground black pepper

Often the simplest flavors are the strongest. Here, the pairing of lemon and salt works perfectly when applied lightly to the rib roast. It also works well when paired with the Country Sourdough (page 210) and Bone Marrow Mashed Potatoes (page 175).

In a small bowl, thoroughly combine all the ingredients. Rub on the meat about 1 hour before you plan to grill, and then store the leftover rub in the refrigerator for up to 1 week.

LEMON-PARSLEY MARINADE

2 medium lemons, juiced

2 garlic cloves, finely chopped

¼ cup fresh parsley, finely chopped

¼ cup fresh basil, finely chopped

1 tablespoon red bell pepper, finely chopped

1 tablespoon coarsely ground black pepper

2 teaspoons fresh sea salt

½ cup extra-virgin olive oil

Spoon this light marinade around the prime rib. Massage some of the parsley into the meat so that it will be absorbed when roasting.

1. In a medium bowl, combine all the ingredients and let rest for 15 minutes so the flavors can spread throughout the marinade.

2. Add the rib roast to the marinade. Transfer to the refrigerator and let marinate for about 4 hours. If the marinade does not fully cover the meat, turn the meat halfway through the marinating process so that all areas of the meat receive equal amounts of the marinade.

OLIVE OIL & GARLIC MARINADE

12 garlic cloves, crushed

6 sprigs fresh rosemary, leaves removed

4 sprigs fresh thyme, leaves removed

2½ cups extra-virgin olive oil

1 tablespoon coarsely ground black pepper

1 tablespoon fresh sea salt

Two of the most fundamental flavors when it comes to home cooking and prime rib, there's not much more to say on this one other than you'll enjoy it.

1. Add all the ingredients to a bowl large enough to hold the rib roast. Transfer the marinade into the refrigerator and let stand for about 45 minutes.

2. Add the rib roast to the marinade and let marinate for 2 hours in the refrigerator. Note that the rib roast will not be fully submerged in the marinade, so be sure to rotate it throughout the marinating process so that all sides of the roast receive equal marinating time.

3. A half hour before roasting, remove the prime rib from the marinade and place on a roasting rack so that the marinade seeps from the meat.

WORCESTERSHIRE MARINADE

¼ cup Worcestershire sauce

2 tablespoons fresh rosemary, finely chopped

4 garlic cloves, diced

1 tablespoon coarsely ground black pepper

1 tablespoon fresh sea salt

Use this marinade when cooking it up for the boys—the Worcestershire always keeps them coming back for seconds. This marinade is great when prepared with either the B&B or One-Pot technique (pages 125 and 112), and serve along-side some Spiced Corn (page 199) and Brussels Sprouts with Charred Bacon (page 193).

1. In a small bowl, combine all the ingredients.

2. When the rib roast has been seasoned and placed on a roasting rack, pierce deep holes into the meat with a carving fork.

3. Next, slowly pour the Worcestershire marinade over the rib roast so that it seeps into the piercings in the meat. Baste periodically throughout the roasting process.

RED WINE & DIJON MARINADE

¾ cup dry red wine

¼ cup extra-virgin olive oil

2 garlic cloves, minced

1 tablespoon Dijon mustard

1 tablespoon coarsely ground black pepper

1 tablespoon fresh sea salt

1 teaspoon fresh rosemary, finely chopped

Red wine and prime rib often go hand in hand, and I love applying this marinade to my prime ribs for special occasions. I encourage you to go with a nicer bottle of red wine here, and be sure to set aside a little for dinner since those flavors in the warm prime rib will be complemented perfectly with your chosen wine. Maybe even save a little Dijon and place it on the side of your plate so that you use it on several bites of your prime rib.

1. Add all the ingredients to a bowl large enough to hold the rib roast. Transfer the marinade into the refrigerator and let stand for about 45 minutes.

2. Next, add the rib roast to the marinade and let marinate for 2 hours in the refrigerator. Note that the rib roast will not be fully submerged in the marinade, so be sure to rotate it throughout the marinating process in order for all sides of the roast to receive equal marinating time.

3. A half hour before roasting, remove the prime rib from the marinade and place on a roasting rack so that the marinade seeps from the meat.

4. While cooking, baste the roast with the remaining marinade about every 30 minutes.

CITRUS MARINADE

¾ cup orange juice

½ medium lime, juiced

½ medium lemon, juiced

¼ cup cilantro, finely chopped

¼ cup extra-virgin olive oil

2 tablespoons fresh rosemary, finely chopped

4 garlic cloves, minced

1 tablespoon coarsely ground black pepper

1 tablespoon fresh sea salt

This recipe is grounded in the essential citrus flavors: orange, lemon, and lime. You'll be surprised just how good this prime rib comes out.

1. Add all the ingredients to a bowl large enough to hold the rib roast. Transfer the marinade into the refrigerator and let stand for about 45 minutes.

2. Next, add the rib roast to the marinade and let marinate for 2 hours in the refrigerator. Note that the rib roast will not be fully submerged in the marinade, so be sure to rotate it throughout the marinating process in order for all sides of the roast to receive equal marinating time.

3. A half hour before roasting, remove the prime rib from the marinade and place on a roasting rack so that the marinade seeps from the meat. Discard the remaining marinade.

CILANTRO-LIME MARINADE

2 limes, juiced

¼ cup extra-virgin olive oil

¼ cup fresh cilantro, finely chopped

2 garlic cloves, finely chopped

2 teaspoons coarsely ground black pepper

2 teaspoons fresh sea salt

½ teaspoon organic honey

Cilantro is one of my favorite herbs, and I love it on or alongside nearly every cut of meat.

1. In a medium bowl or roasting pan, combine all the ingredients and let rest for 15 minutes so the flavors can spread throughout the marinade.

2. Add your desired meat to the marinade. Transfer to the refrigerator and let marinate from 4 hours to overnight. If the marinade does not fully cover the meat, turn the meat halfway through the marinating process so that all areas of the meat receive equal amounts of the marinade.

LEMON-ROSEMARY MARINADE

4 lemons, halved and juiced

6 garlic cloves

3 sprigs fresh thyme, leaves removed

3 sprigs fresh rosemary, leaves removed

2 teaspoons ground fennel seeds

1 tablespoon coarsely ground black pepper

1 tablespoon fresh sea salt

The lemon is packed with such a strong kick. But this marinade is not the most voluminous, so be sure to ladle it all around the marinade.

1. In a medium bowl, combine all the ingredients and let rest for 15 minutes so the flavors can spread throughout the marinade.

2. Add the rib roast to the marinade. Transfer to the refrigerator and let marinate for about 4 hours. If the marinade does not fully cover the meat, turn the meat halfway through the marinating process so that all areas of the meat receive equal amounts of the marinade

PRIME RIB

A RIB ROAST IS ONE OF THE MOST COMMON CUTS OF MEAT TO PREPARE ON A SPECIAL OCCASION OR HOLIDAY, THOUGH IN MY OPINION, IT SHOULD BE PREPARED MUCH MORE OFTEN. For about as long as I can remember, my mother has always prepared her rib roast on any occasion she deemed fitting—from Christmas Eve to the occasion of my first job, I could always count on a rib roast being served that very evening. Though, in all fairness, my mother prepares her rib roast in the gentlest way, making it look effortless. Every Christmas morning, just after we exchange our gifts one by one, she makes her way to the kitchen, a mug of coffee with cream in her hand, and slowly begins to prepare her rib roast that she had purchased days in advance.

Never once have I ever I heard her complain about the diligence that is involved in her preparation of the roast, and she serves baked potatoes, asparagus, and rolls with it. My father and uncle always get the ends—though there's typically some dispute involved—and we joke about letting our belts out a notch to make room for the roast. But once we start eating, we're unusually quiet, appreciating all the flavors and textures and eventually making our way in for seconds and sometimes thirds. "The best compliment is your silence," Mom has said with a laugh. The truth is, there is no rib roast recipe that's quite like my mother's—but now that I think about it, this seems to be the case with nearly everything she does! As such, it's only fair that the first recipe in this section be attributed to her.

A classic rib roast has a rather simple recipe when it comes to its preparation. With nearly all the recipes in this book, the active time involved in preparing the dinner is just about 1 hour. The roasting process is ultimately the time consumed in its preparation—usually we're dealing with about 3 to 4 hours until the internal temperature of the roast is about 125 degrees for medium-rare.

While the roast cooks in the oven, there are several elements to it that you should keep in mind. First, you want your roast to be succulent and juicy so that while it's cooking it will release its juices naturally, which will then accumulate at the bottom of the pan, along with browned pieces from the roast that'll give the juice, which can later be turned into an au jus, an extra kick of flavor.

To get the juices to slowly drip from the roast, we usually turn down the roasting temperature to 325 degrees after the roast's initial searing at 450; this encourages a slower roasting process, allowing the blood and fat in the meat to naturally come together and seep out of the roast. You should also always be aware of the crust on the outside of the roast.

To account for a slightly crisp outer layer, we always place the roast in the oven at 450 so that the instant heat strikes the roast (which should always be at room temperature), it is seared so that its cap becomes crisp. After the initial searing, if you start to notice that the crust is becoming too crisp for your liking, place a sheet of aluminum foil gently on top of the roast so that it traps in the moisture.

Although very few of my roasts will ever bring back the memories that my mother's brings, they are all great for different occasions. Be sure to season your roast generously, and don't be afraid to add select elements of your own to the seasoning. Roasting for 3 to 4 hours will change the immediate flavors of your seasoning, usually gently accounting for the flavors in the cap of the meat.

MOM'S PERFECT PRIME RIB

MAKES 6 TO 8 SERVINGS
ACTIVE TIME: 1 HOUR
TOTAL TIME: 5 HOURS

1 6-rib rib roast with ribs removed

5 medium garlic cloves, crushed into a fine paste

3 tablespoons fresh sea salt, coarse if possible

4 tablespoons coarsely ground black pepper

6 bunches fresh rosemary

6 bunches fresh thyme

My mother has made her prime rib on practically every holiday since I was a kid, and I must admit, this is by far my favorite way to eat it. With four men sitting around the table, not a word is said while we slowly make our way through her rib roast, always served with charred asparagus and a baked potato with sour cream and chives. Because of her technique, it's a toss-up who will get the end piece. My dad always has one (this is a golden rule in my house!) and my brothers and I have to sweet talk mom into saving the other for us! If this is the case for you, you can always cut the roast in half before transferring to the oven to give you four ends—this has happened recently at my mother's house, given that we all want that end piece!

1. Remove the rib roast from the refrigerator 30 minutes before cooking and let stand at room temperature. Preheat the oven to 450 degrees.

2. Generously apply the garlic paste onto the meat side and both ends of the prime rib, followed by half the fresh sea salt and coarsely ground pepper.

3. Chop 1 bunch of rosemary and 1 bunch of thyme and place in a small bowl. Mix with the rest of the salt and pepper. Press the herb mixture against the side of the meat so it sticks.

4. Place a roasting rack in the center of a roasting pan. Take the remaining rosemary and thyme bunches and set on the rack so that they form a bed, alternating the rosemary and thyme.

5. Place the roast meat-side down onto the herb-covered rack.

6. Place the roast in the oven and cook for 20 minutes; then lower temperature to 325 degrees. Cook the roast for about 3 to 4 more hours until internal temperature reaches 130 degrees.

7. Remove the roast from the oven, transfer to a large carving board, and let stand for about 15 minutes before carving.

PRIME RIB AU POIVRE

MAKES 6 TO 8 SERVINGS
ACTIVE TIME: 1 HOUR AND
30 MINUTES
TOTAL TIME: 4 HOURS

1 6-rib rib roast

3 medium garlic cloves, finely chopped

2 tablespoons Dijon mustard

3 to 4 tablespoons whole black peppercorns

1 tablespoon fresh sea salt

3 bunches fresh rosemary (optional)

The au poivre works well when served on select red meats. Today you can find a Filet Mignon au Poivre at nearly every steakhouse. At its most fundamental recipe, the au poivre style simply requires you to heavily pepper your meat so that its sharp, spicy flavors enter the meat at a shallow level. Likewise, because the flavors are so heavy and powerful, the au poivre style works perfectly on meats that have a relatively small surface area, such as the filet mignon or prime rib. The cap of the prime rib, or the fatty outer rim of the rib roast, is easily permeated with flavor that goes perfectly with the au poivre technique. To add a little bit of a flair to this recipe, I've included a Dijon-garlic paste as a base layer to the au poivre, broadening the flavors.

1. Remove the rib roast from the refrigerator 1 hour before cooking and let stand at room temperature.

2. Preheat the oven to 325 degrees.

3. Mix the garlic and Dijon mustard in a small bowl so that it forms a paste. Next, when the meat's temperature has lowered, generously apply the paste to the meat side of the prime rib. Use your hands so that the mustard will spread into the prime rib's cap.

4. Place the whole black peppercorns in a small, sealable bag and seal tightly. Place the bag on a flat surface and then, using the bottom of a heavy pan such as a cast-iron skillet, firmly pound the peppercorns so that they split into large pieces—much more coarse than what a traditional pepper mill will give you. Remove the split peppercorns from the bag and mix in a small bowl with the fresh sea salt.

5. Using your hands, generously pat the split peppercorns and fresh sea salt onto the prime rib already rubbed with the Dijon-garlic paste. If you want to add a rosemary element to the prime rib, divide the bunches of rosemary evenly and place in between the ribs; tie firmly with butcher's twine so that the rosemary stays in place while roasting.

6. Transfer the au poivre prime rib onto a large rack set in a roasting pan. Transfer the rib roast to the oven and cook for 2½ to 3 hours, until a thermometer registers 125 degrees for medium-rare. During the roasting process, the crust of the rib roast may begin to brown; if so, gently cover it with a sheet of aluminum foil in order to help maintain the moisture of the crust.

7. Remove the rib roast from the oven, transfer to a large carving board, and let stand for about 10 minutes before carving.

TIP: YOU CAN USE THE JUICES LEFT OVER IN THE ROASTING PAN FOR AN AU JUS, IF YOU LIKE IT VERY PEPPERY. IN THAT CASE, DOUBLE THE AMOUNT OF RED WINE AND BEEF BROTH USED IN THE RECIPE, MAINTAINING A 1:2 RATIO.

ROTISSERIE-GRILLED PRIME RIB

MAKES 6 TO 8 SERVINGS
ACTVE TIME: 1 HOUR AND
15 MINUTES
TOTAL TIME: 4 HOURS

A 6-rib rib roast

3 tablespoons extra-virgin olive oil

4 garlic cloves, minced

1 small shallot, finely chopped

2 tablespoons coarse sea salt

2 tablespoons coarsely ground black pepper

3 bunches fresh thyme

3 bunches fresh rosemary

2 cups hickory or maple woodchips

The rotisserie is a great tool on a summer evening for a quick prime rib. One of my favorite elements to this meal is that its timing is extremely easy: only 16 to 18 minutes per pound of meat. When you rotisserie the meat, the constant, slow turning of the meat ensures it will receive equal amounts of heat, which quickens the cooking process. Be sure to place an aluminum pan under the rib roast as it is cooking to catch the juices that will fall out; they can be used for a Basic Au Jus (page 133).

1. Rub the rib roast with 1 tablespoon of the extra-virgin olive oil and let rest at room temperature for 1 hour.

2. In a small bowl, combine the minced garlic and finely chopped shallot with the remaining extra-virgin olive oil. Generously massage the meat with the garlic-shallot purée so that it clings to the cap of the rib roast.

3. Season the rib roast generously with the coarsely ground black pepper and fresh sea salt. Take the bunches of thyme and rosemary and evenly distribute them between the ribs. With butcher's twine, tie the bunches of herbs tightly around the ends of the ribs so that they will stay in place when you rotisserie the roast. Let the rib roast stand for 30 minutes while preparing the gas grill.

4. Preheat the gas grill to 250 degrees.

5. Add the hickory or maple woodchips to a small bowl filled with water and let soak. Set alongside the grill.

6. Spit the rib roast with the rotisserie's prongs so that the spit goes through the center of the rib roast toward the bone. I recommend trussing the rib roast with butcher's twine around the spit as an extra precaution.

6. Set a large aluminum roasting pan on the grill and then place the rib roast on the rotisserie above the pan, so that the juices will fall into the dish (see page 130 for au jus guidelines).

7. Cover the grill and roast the prime rib at a low speed for about 2½ hours (16 to 18 minutes per pound, to be more exact). At this point, an instant read thermometer should record the internal heat as below 125 degrees.

8. Now, heat the smoking box and when hot, throw a handful of woodchips into the heat periodically so that you continuously smoke the prime rib while it finishes roasting—about another 30 minutes, until the thermometer reads 125 degrees.

9. Remove the rib roast from the rotisserie and transfer to a large carving board. Let stand for 10 minutes before carving, allowing the meat to properly store its juices.

CHARCOAL PIT PRIME RIB

MAKES 6 TO 8 SERVINGS
**ACTIVE TIME: 1 HOUR AND
30 MINUTES**
TOTAL TIME: 4 HOURS

1 6-rib rib roast

3 tablespoons extra-
virgin olive oil

2 tablespoons coarsely
ground black pepper

2 tablespoons coarse
sea salt

4 garlic cloves, minced

3 bunches fresh thyme

3 bunches fresh
rosemary

When working with charcoal, you'll obtain an authentic taste of grilling to your prime rib. Here it's important to note that the roasting temperature is just 325 degrees and the total roasting time is a little more than 2 hours.

1. Rub the rib roast with 1 tablespoon of the extra-virgin olive oil and let rest at room temperature for 30 minutes.

2. Season the rib roast generously with the coarsely ground black pepper and fresh sea salt.

3. In a small bowl, combine the minced garlic and the remaining extra-virgin olive oil, and then massage this marinade into the meat side of the rib roast. Take the bunches of thyme and rosemary and evenly distribute between the ribs. With butcher's twine, tie the bunches of herbs tightly around the ribs so that they will stay in place when you flip the meat on the grill. Let stand for 30 minutes while preparing the charcoal grill.

4. Prepare the charcoal grill to medium-low heat.

5. When the grill is ready, at about 325 degrees with the coals lightly covered with ash, place the rib roast in the middle of the grill and sear each side, including the ends, for about 2 to 3 minutes each. Next, flip the rib roast so that the bone-side is pressed against the rack, and then slowly roast for about 2 hours until the rib roast is charred and an instant thermometer reads 125 degrees. You'll need to restock the pit with charcoals to maintain an even roasting temperature of 325 degrees.

6. Remove the rib roast from the grill and transfer to a large carving board. Let stand for 10 minutes before carving, allowing the meat to properly store its juices.

TIP: KEEP A KEEN EYE ON YOUR FIRE PIT, MAKING SURE THAT YOUR COOKING TEMPERATURE REMAINS CONSISTENT AND YOUR COALS ARE GIVING OFF JUST ENOUGH SMOKE SO THAT IT WON'T OVERPOWER THE MEAT.

SLOW-COOKER PRIME RIB

MAKES 4 SERVINGS
ACTIVE TIME: 1 HOUR
TOTAL TIME: 6 HOURS

A 3- or 4-rib rib roast

2 tablespoons coarsely ground black pepper

2 tablespoons fresh sea salt

4 garlic cloves, minced

1 teaspoon extra-virgin olive oil

4 sprigs fresh rosemary

4 sprigs fresh thyme

1 cup dry red wine (preferably one you plan on serving at dinner)

1 cup chicken stock

1 bay leaf

The simplicity of this recipe makes it perfect for afternoons when you just don't have the time to stand around and prepare a traditional full-course meal. With the slow cooker, a low temperature cooks the meat over a longer period of time, requiring little to no effort. Even here, when we consider the dry red wine and chicken stock that the prime rib cooks in for 5 hours, it's not entirely necessary to baste the roast every 30 minutes. Instead, just make sure that everything gets into the roast and that you cook it on the low setting. Other than that, just let the slow cooker do all the work for you.

1. Remove the rib roast from the refrigerator 1 hour before cooking. Using your hands, thoroughly apply the coarsely ground black pepper and fresh sea salt to the rib roast.

2. Next, in a small bowl, mix together the minced garlic and extra-virgin olive oil, and then apply to the roast. Let the roast stand at room temperature for about 1 hour.

3. Add the rosemary, thyme, red wine, chicken stock, and bay leaf to a slow cooker. Add the rib roast, fat side up, to the slow cooker. Turn the slow cooker to low and let cook for about 5 hours until, when tested with an instant-read thermometer, the internal temperature reads 130 degrees for medium-rare. Note that the marinade will not completely submerge the rib roast, so baste it or flip the meat halfway through the cooking time.

4. Remove the rib roast from the slow cooker and place on a large carving board. Let rest for 15 minutes before carving. As far as the leftover marinade goes, you can use this as the base of a sauce or gravy (see the Sauces & Gravies introduction on page 132 for basic instructions on how to build your own sauce).

WOOD-FIRED PRIME RIB

MAKES 6 TO 8 SERVINGS
ACTIVE TIME: 1 HOUR AND 30 MINUTES
TOTAL TIME: 4 HOURS

A 6-rib rib roast

3 tablespoons extra-virgin olive oil

4 garlic cloves, minced

1 small shallot, finely chopped

2 tablespoons coarse sea salt

2 tablespoons coarsely ground black pepper

3 bunches fresh thyme

3 bunches fresh rosemary

While grilling a rib roast over a wood fire, you'll want to be sure that the smoke does not directly rise up to the rib roast because that will give it too much of a smoky flavor. To combat this, you may want to set up the grill so that it features both direct and indirect heating. Simply stock your wood on one side of the fire pit and then place the rib roast towards the middle of the grilling rack. The area directly above the fire is your "direct" heating zone, and the area on the opposite side that is still hot, though does not receive the same level of flame, will be your "indirect" zone.

1. Rub the rib roast with 1 tablespoon of the extra-virgin olive oil and let rest at room temperature for 1 hour.

2. In a small bowl, combine the minced garlic and finely chopped shallot with the remaining extra-virgin olive oil. After the rib roast has rested at room temperature for about an hour, lowering the internal temperature of the meat so that it takes on flavors more easily, generously massage the meat with the garlic-shallot purée so that it clings to the cap of the rib roast.

3. Season the rib roast generously with the coarsely ground black pepper and fresh sea salt. Take the bunches of thyme and rosemary and evenly distribute between the ribs. With butcher's twine, tie the bunches of herbs tightly around the ribs so that they will stay in place when you flip the meat on the grill. Once again, let the rib roast stand for 30 minutes while preparing the charcoal grill.

4. Prepare the wood fire to feature both direct and indirect heating at an average medium-low heat of about 325 degrees. You'll want to make sure that you have a strong foundational layer of coals so that you can easily maintain the heat and smoke as you grill your prime rib.

5. When the fire is ready, at about 325 degrees with the logs lightly covered with ash, place the rib roast towards the middle of the grill (in between both heating zones, away from the smoke) and sear each side, including the ends, for about 2 to 3 minutes each. Next, flip the rib roast so that the bone-side is pressed against the rack, and then slowly roast for about 2 hours until the rib roast is charred and an instant thermometer reads 125 degrees.

6. Remove the rib roast from the grill and transfer to a large carving board. Let stand for 10 minutes before carving, allowing the meat to properly store its juices.

TIP: THE CHOICE OF WOOD YOU USE FOR YOUR FIRE IS ALWAYS ESSENTIAL TO THE GRILLING FLAVOR OF YOUR MEAT. FOR A MORE MEDIUM LEVEL OF FLAVOR, GO WITH A HICKORY OR OAK WOOD, GIVING YOUR RIB ROAST JUST THE RIGHT AMOUNT OF SMOKE FLAVOR. IF YOU'D LIKE MORE OF A KICK TO YOUR RIB ROAST, ADD A LOG OR TWO OF MESQUITE ONTO A FIRE THAT'S ALREADY ROOTED WITH HICKORY OR MAPLE WOOD.

SMOKED PRIME RIB

MAKES 6 TO 8 SERVINGS
ACTIVE TIME: 2 HOURS
TOTAL TIME: 6 HOURS

A 6-rib rib roast

3 tablespoons extra-virgin olive oil

4 garlic cloves, minced

1 small shallot, finely chopped

2 tablespoons coarse sea salt

2 tablespoons coarsely ground black pepper

3 bunches fresh thyme

3 bunches fresh rosemary

4 cups hickory or maple woodchips

The key to a properly smoked rib roast lies in the fire. As with the Wood-Fired Prime Rib, the woodchips you chose will greatly influence the flavor of your meat. Be sure to soak your woodchips for about an hour before using on the grill, and after dispersing on top of the coals, cover the grill and align the air vent away from the fire so that the smoke will build underneath the lid and pillow over the meat. If you'd like more of a barbecued smoke flavor—perfect for summer evenings—mix 1 cup of mesquite woodchips with 2 cups of hickory or maple woodchips and then soak before throwing onto the flames.

1. Rub the rib roast with 1 tablespoon of the extra-virgin olive oil and let rest at room temperature for 1 hour.

2. In a small bowl, combine the minced garlic and finely chopped shallot with the 2 remaining tablespoons of extra-virgin olive oil. After the rib roast has rested at room temperature for about an hour, lowering the internal temperature of the meat so that it takes on flavors more easily, generously massage the meat with the garlic-shallot purée so that it clings to the cap of the rib roast.

3. Season the rib roast generously with the coarsely ground black pepper and fresh sea salt. Take the bunches of thyme and rosemary and evenly distribute between the ribs. With butcher's twine, tie the bunches of herbs tightly around the ribs so that they will stay in place when you flip the meat on the grill. Let the rib roast stand for 30 minutes while preparing the charcoal grill.

4. Prepare the fire to feature both direct and indirect heat with an average low temperature of about 300 degrees. You'll want to make sure that you have a strong foundational layer of coals so that you can easily maintain the heat and smoke as you grill your prime rib. While you prepare your grill, add the 4 cups of hickory or maple woodchips to a bowl of warm water and set aside.

5. When the fire is ready, at about 300 degrees with the coals lightly covered with ash, place the rib roast over the direct heat of the grill and sear each side, including the ends, for about 2 to 3 minutes each. Transfer the rib roast over the direct heat and flip the rib roast to meat side up. Take a handful of woodchips and throw them over the flame. Cover the grill, aligning the air vent away from flame so that the smoke pillows around the rib roast, and begin slowly roasting for about 3 to 4 hours until the rib roast is charred and an instant thermometer reads 125 degrees. For the first 3 hours of the grilling process, distribute handfuls of the hickory or maple woodchips about every 30 minutes or so.

6. Remove the rib roast from the grill and transfer to a large carving board. Let stand for 10 minutes before carving, allowing the meat to properly store its juices.

ONE-POT PRIME RIB

MAKES 6 TO 8 SERVINGS
ACTIVE TIME: 1 HOUR AND 30 MINUTES
TOTAL TIME: 6 HOURS

A 4-rib rib roast, frenched (see instructions on page 120)

2 tablespoons coarsely ground black pepper

2 tablespoons fresh sea salt

1 tablespoon, plus 1 teaspoon extra-virgin olive oil

2 bunches fresh rosemary

2 bunches fresh thyme

12 large carrots, peeled and chopped into 2-inch segments

2 large white onions, diced

8 medium russet potatoes

1 cup dry red wine

1½ cups beef broth

1 bay leaf

Here, technique is key. This prime rib is structured on a simple recipe that will give you a full meal all in one. You'll need a large Dutch oven, or a large roasting pan will work as well. Essentially, what you put into the prime rib depends on your mood and what type of sides you want—though here, I'm provided my favorite side dishes of Baked Asparagus and soft potatoes, onions, and carrots glazed with the red wine and juices from the prime rib. For the red wine base, try a full-body red wine recommended on pages 66 through 73. And pour a glass for yourself.

1. Remove the rib roast from the refrigerator 1 hour before cooking. Using your hands, thoroughly apply the coarsely ground black pepper and fresh sea salt to the rib roast.

2. Next, in a small bowl, mix together the minced garlic and 1 teaspoon of the extra-virgin olive oil, and then apply to the roast. Break apart the rosemary and thyme bunches into quarters and then evenly distribute the sprigs between the bones on the top of the roast. With butcher's twine, tie the herbs firmly to the roast. Let the roast stand at room temperature for about 1 hour.

3. Prepare the oven to 425 degrees.

4. Place a small roasting rack in the Dutch oven or roasting pan (note: if you don't have a rack that will fit in the Dutch oven, simply line the bottom of the pot with several sheets of aluminum foil.) Next, space a sheet or two of aluminum foil evenly across the roasting rack, and then place the Dutch oven or roasting pan in the oven while it heats.

5. Place the carrots, onions, and potatoes in the bottom of the Dutch oven or roasting pan. Next, add the wine, beef broth, and bay leaf to the pan and stir thoroughly. Place the rib roast on the roasting rack and then transfer to the Dutch oven or roasting pan in the oven and cook for 15 minutes at 425 degrees so that the roast gets a good initial searing. Reduce the heat to 325 degrees and cook for another 3 to 4 hours, until the middle of the roast reads 125 degrees if tested with an instant-read thermometer.

6. A half hour before removing the roast from the oven, place the asparagus in a small baking dish, coat with the remaining extra-virgin olive oil, season with the coarsely ground black pepper and fresh sea salt, and then place in the oven and bake until browned, about 20 to 30 minutes. When finished, remove and cover with aluminum.

7. Remove the roast from the oven and let stand for 15 minutes before carving. Using a large slotted-spoon, remove the soft carrots, onions, and potatoes from the broth and let drain in a strainer. Serve warm with Baked Asparagus (page 171).

GLUTEN FREE GF

COWBOY STEAKS

MAKES 2 TO 3 SERVINGS
ACTIVE TIME: 15 MINUTES
TOTAL TIME: 1 HOUR AND 30 MINUTES

2 bone-in rib eye steaks, about 1¼ to 1½ inches thick, cut from rib roast

2 tablespoons extra-virgin olive oil

Coarsely ground black pepper

Fresh sea salt

Traditional rib eye steaks come straight from the rib roast. Because the prime rib is nearly always roasted (even when it's grilled, it undergoes the roasting technique), the meat develops a much richer flavor and a softer, tender consistency. However, when you slice the rib eye directly between the ribs, you'll receive a bone-in rib eye, or a classic cowboy steak. Grilling the rib eye scores the meat quickly over the flames of the grill, allowing the meat to have a tough, grainy texture that is unique to the rib eye altogether.

1. Rub both sides of the steaks with the extra-virgin olive oil and let rest at room temperature for about 1 hour.

2. A half hour before cooking, prepare the gas or charcoal grill to medium-high heat.

3. When the grill is ready, about 400 to 450 degrees with the coals lightly covered with ash, season one side of the steaks with half of the coarsely ground pepper and sea salt. Place the seasoned sides of the steaks on the grill and cook for about 6 to 7 minutes, until blood begins to rise from the tops. Season the tops of the steaks while you wait.

4. When the steaks are charred, flip and cook for 4 to 5 more minutes for medium-rare and 5 to 6 more minutes for medium. The steaks should feel slightly firm if poked in the center. (I recommend cooking the rib eye to medium; medium-rare will be very chewy and tough. For a boneless rib eye, cook for 2 to 4 minutes less.)

5. Remove the steaks from the grill and transfer to a large cutting board. Let stand for 5 to 10 minutes, allowing the steaks to properly store their juices and flavor.

TIP: THE RIB EYE IS OFTEN BARBEQUED WITH RUBS AND MARINADES, THOUGH I TEND TO FIND IT BEST WHEN SERVED WITH A CHIMICHURRI SAUCE (PAGE 15 FOR ARGENTINIAN CHIMICHURRI OR PAGE 147 FOR FARM-STYLE CHIMICHURRI).

BEER-MARINATED PRIME RIB

MAKES 6 TO 8 SERVINGS
ACTIVE TIME: 1 HOUR AND 30 MINUTES
TOTAL TIME: 6 HOURS

A 6-rib rib roast

3 tablespoons coarsely ground black pepper

2 tablespoons fresh sea salt

4 garlic cloves, minced

¼ cup, plus 2 teaspoons extra-virgin olive oil

4 sprigs fresh rosemary

4 sprigs fresh thyme

2 tablespoons soy sauce

1 teaspoon Worcestershire sauce

2 cups dark beer (brown ale, dark stout, etc.)

1 large white onion, diced

In the summer time, beer is the perfect marinade for any cut of red meat. Though traditionally, rib roasts aren't marinated with beer too often—hence the reason this recipe originally comes from a marinade I prepared for a couple Cowboy Steaks (page 114). Since the rib roast has a dense core, the marinade will mostly penetrate the roast's cap, with a little flavor making its way to the core. For this recipe, I encourage you to try it toward the end of fall, and serve it with a porter or stout.

1. Place the rib roast meat side down in a large bowl or baking pan—something large enough to hold the rib roast. Next, generously season the meat with the coarsely ground black pepper and fresh sea salt, massaging it in with your hands and making sure that the seasoning thoroughly sticks to the roast.

2. Mix the minced garlic and the 2 teaspoons of the extra-virgin olive oil in a small cup, and then brush onto the rib roast over the pepper and salt.

3. Add the remaining ingredients into the baking pan and mix thoroughly. Note that the entire rib roast will not be submerged in the marinade—part of the reason why we want to keep the rib roast meat side down in the baking pan—so be sure to spoon the marinade onto the rib side of the roast throughout the marinating process.

4. Transfer the baking dish into the refrigerator and let marinate for about 4 hours. Remove roast from the marinade and transfer to a large carving board 1 hour before roasting. Set the marinade aside; it will be used for basting during the roasting process.

5. Preheat the oven to 425 degrees.

6. Place the rib roast meat side up on a rack in the roasting pan. Lightly season again with the coarsely ground black pepper and fresh sea salt. When the oven is ready, transfer the rib roast to the oven and cook for 15 minutes at 450 degrees so that it gets a strong initial searing.

7. Reduce the heat to 325 degrees and continue to roast for about 3 to 4 more hours. Baste with the marinade every 30 minutes or so during the roasting process. Use the juices and marinade that accumulate at the bottom of the roasting pan as a strong base for an au jus (page 133).

8. Remove the rib roast from the oven and let stand for 15 minutes before carving, allowing it to properly store its juices and flavor.

TIP: TO MAKE THIS DISH GLUTEN-FREE, USE GLUTEN-FREE BEER AND CHECK THE LABEL ON YOUR WORCESTERSHIRE SAUCE.

FRENCHED PRIME RIB

MAKES 6 TO 8 SERVINGS
ACTIVE TIME: 2 HOURS
TOTAL TIME: 6 HOURS

A 6-rib rib roast

2 tablespoons coarse
sea salt

2 tablespoons coarsely
ground black pepper

¼ cup extra-
virgin olive oil

6 garlic cloves, minced

1 tablespoon chopped
fresh thyme, plus 3
bunches

1 tablespoon chopped
fresh rosemary, plus 3
bunches

Frenching a cut of meat isn't too challenging and is normally done when serving to impress. Essentially, when you french a cut of meat, you trim the meat away from the upper portion of the bones so that when roasted, the bones flare out at the top in an elegant fashion. To french, all you need is a sharp carving knife and paring knife in order to remove the meat from the bones. As seen in the recipe, I encourage you to tie bunches of thyme and rosemary into the spaces between the bones for an extra bit of flavor and fashion!

1. Remove the rib roast from the refrigerator and place on cooling racks over a large carving board, bone side down. In order to french the rib roast, you will need to cut off the meat that is on top of the bones. To do so, go about 2 inches down the ribs and using a carving knife, cut down through the meat until you reach the bone. Make a sharp cut and then cut up the bone so that the top of the meat can be peeled off. This top meat is very delicate and flavorful and works great in stews.

2. Stand the rib roast up and starting with the left bone, cut down 1 to 2 inches along the bone, cut across to the next bone, and then cut back up so that you get a rectangular chunk of the meat to come apart from the space between the ribs. Do this to all the ribs, and then gently cut away the meat so that the ribs are left to stand openly and on their own. Using a paring knife, gently scrape away any bits of meat that still cling to the ribs. Set roast aside.

3. In a small bowl, combine the 2 tablespoons of coarse sea salt and coarsely ground black pepper. Using your hands, massage the seasoning into the rib roast so that the grains of salt and pepper cling to it firmly.

4. Next, in a small bowl, whisk together the extra-virgin olive oil and minced garlic, followed by the finely chopped thyme and rosemary. Brush the marinade over the rib roast, making sure that the majority of the finely chopped herbs are applied to the ends of the roast. Let the roast stand for about 30 minutes to 1 hour while you preheat the oven.

5. Preheat the oven to 450 degrees.

6. Using some butcher's twine, carefully tie the thyme and rosemary bunches into the spaces between the ribs so that they are firmly in place. Place the roast rib side down, meat side up on a rack in a large roasting pan. When the oven is ready, transfer the rib roast to the oven and cook for 15 minutes at 450 degrees so that the rib roast gets a strong initial searing. Reduce the heat to 325 degrees and continue to roast for about 3 to 4 more hours.

7. Toward the end of the recommended roasting time, use an instant-read thermometer to check the internal temperature of the meat. When it reads 125 degrees, pull the rib roast out for medium-rare.

8. Let the rib roast stand at room temperature for 10 minutes before carving, allowing it to properly store its juices and flavor.

CROWNED ROAST OF BEEF

MAKES 12 SERVINGS
ACTIVE TIME: 2 HOURS
TOTAL TIME: 5 HOURS

A 10-rib rib roast

3 tablespoons coarsely ground black pepper

3 tablespoons fresh sea salt

1 cup extra-virgin olive oil

8 garlic cloves, minced

⅓ cup fresh thyme, coarsely chopped

⅓ cup fresh rosemary, coarsely chopped

4 tablespoons fresh sage, finely chopped

Although crowning a roast of meat is traditionally done more often for roasts of pork and lamb, you can also crown a roast of beef. It's a little more challenging and requires you to do so on a larger cut of prime rib—about 10 ribs. Built upon the fundamental method of frenching the meat, a crowned prime rib has the frenched ribs at the top, though it's sliced and bent into a circle so that the ribs, when positioned properly, resemble a crown. Butcher's twine is definitely required here, and the variation allows you to use the space between the roast for a stuffing—though if this is too tight a cavity, simply roast the stuffing in a baking dish for 1 hour until browned.

1. Remove the rib roast from the refrigerator and place it on cooling racks over a large carving board, bone-side down. To begin, you will need to french the rib roast. First, cut the meat that covers the bones. To do so, go about 2 inches down the ribs and using a sharp carving knife, cut through the meat until you reach the bone. Make a sharp cut and then cut up the bone so that the top of the meat can be peeled off.

2. Stand the rib roast up and starting with the left bone, cut down 1 to 2 inches along the bone, across to the next bone, and then back up so that you get a rectangular chunk of the meat to come apart from the space between the ribs. Do this to all the ribs, and then gently cut away the meat so that the ribs are left to stand openly and on their own. Using a paring knife, gently scrape away any bits of meat that still cling to the ribs.

3. Bring the meat together into a circle, cut about ½ to 1 inch into the meat side of the rib roast between each bone. Make your cuts even and leveled. Stand the rib roast and, pushing back the ends of the roast, form it into a tight crown. Note that because it's fairly difficult to crown a roast of beef, you may need to cut deeper than 1 inch between the ribs so that it allows for more flexibility. Using butcher's twine, tie the crown tightly so that it'll remain in that position while roasting—you'll need to tie the roast around the bones themselves, and also around the equator of the roast. Set aside.

4. Mix the coarsely ground black pepper and fresh sea salt in a small bowl. Using your hands, massage the seasoning into the rib roast.

5. In a small bowl whisk together the remaining ingredients. Using your hands, massage the paste into the rib roast. Let stand at room temperature for 30 minutes to 1 hour.

6. Preheat the oven to 450 degrees.

7. Place the standing rib roast in a large roasting pan on a large sheet of flat roasting racks. Cover the crown with aluminum foil so that it keeps the heat central. Roast at 450 degrees for 15 minutes so that the rib roast receives a nice initial searing. Lower the heat to 325 degrees and cook for another 2 to 3 hours, until the internal temperature of the meat reads 125 degrees for medium-rare. Baste the rib roast with its own juices every 30 minutes or so.

8. Remove the crown roast from the oven and place on a large serving piece. Let stand for 10 minutes before carving.

CROWNED ROAST OF BEEF VARIATION:

For a spinach and wild mushroom stuffing to go in the center of the prime rib, follow these instructions:

½ cup (1 stick) unsalted butter

1 pound wild mushrooms (porcini, shiitake, crimini), diced

1 roll Jimmy Dean hot sausage

3 medium garlic cloves, finely chopped

1 large white onion, chopped

4 celery stalks, chopped

¼ cup flat-leaf parsley, coarsely chopped

1 tablespoon fresh rosemary, coarsely chopped

2 teaspoons fresh thyme, coarsely chopped

½ cup fresh baby spinach

3 to 4 cups cubed pieces of day old or lightly-baked Country Sourdough (page 207) or store-bought artisanal bread

1 cup chicken broth

1 large egg

Coarsely ground black pepper

Fresh sea salt

1. Set a medium cast-iron skillet over medium-high heat and add ¼ stick of butter. When hot, add the wild mushrooms to the skillet and cook until tender and browned, about 10 minutes. Remove from pan and set in a large bowl.

2. Next, add the sausage, garlic, white onion, and celery to the skillet and cook until brown, about 5 minutes. You want the sausage to break up into smaller pieces so that it'll mesh thoroughly with the cubed bread. Transfer the sausage mixture to the bowl of mushrooms.

3. Stir the remaining ingredients into the mushroom and sausage mixture and then set aside. When the crowned rib roast has about 1½ hours remaining, remove the aluminum foil from the crown of the rib roast and transfer the stuffing to its center. Season the top with the coarsely ground black pepper and sea salt. Transfer the rib roast back to the oven and cook the rib roast until the internal temperature reads 125 degrees and the stuffing is browned on top.

B&B PRIME RIB DINNER

MAKES 6 TO 8 SERVINGS
ACTIVE TIME: 1 HOUR
TOTAL TIME: 4 HOURS

A 6-rib rib roast

3 tablespoons fresh sea salt

3 tablespoons coarsely ground black pepper

¼ cup extra-virgin olive oil

Josh Capon, executive chef at Burger & Barrel in New York City, serves up the ultimate prime rib dinner. My father and I went there the Monday after the Super Bowl, and we found out that Josh was flying in straight from the Super Bowl in Arizona to serve us our dinner, though it was more like a feast. Served with charred Brussels Sprouts with Charred Bacon (page 193) and Fingerling Potatoes (page 170), this dish is simply extraordinary.

Though the flavors are amazing, the recipe is extremely simple. At B&B, Capon steams his prime rib at 138 degrees for 8 hours, and then sears it on a plancha grill for 15 minutes to give the roast a thick crust. Afterward, he transfers the roast to the oven at an extremely high temperature (450 to 500 degrees, I imagine) and then lets it rest for 10 minutes before serving.

This recipe, based on the meal we experienced at B&B, is adapted slightly to adjust for the steaming process that Josh does. Instead, I initially sear the roast on a plancha skillet or a large cast-iron skillet, and then transfer to the oven at a low heat so that the meat stays as tender as possible.

1. In a small bowl, combine the fresh sea salt and coarsely ground black pepper and mix thoroughly. Using your hands, pat the seasoning firmly onto the rib roast and then brush with the extra-virgin olive oil. Let stand at room temperature for 1 hour before cooking.

2. Set a large plancha skillet across two burners on the stovetop and set to high heat. (You may also use a cast-iron skillet large enough to fit the rib roast.) Place the rib roast fatty side down on the plancha skillet and sear for 15 minutes, until a crust is formed. When crusted, remove from the skillet and place on cooling racks set over a large carving board. Let rest for 15 minutes.

3. Preheat the oven to 325 degrees.

4. Place the rib roast meat side up on a rack in a roasting pan and transfer to the oven. Roast for 2 to 3 hours, basting every 30 minutes or so with its own juices, until its internal temperature reads 125 degrees for medium-rare.

5. Remove the rib roast from the oven and let rest for 10 minutes before carving, allowing it to properly store its juices and flavor.

CALIFORNIAN COFFEE PRIME RIB

MAKES 6 TO 8 SERVINGS
ACTIVE TIME: 1 HOUR
TOTAL TIME: 4 HOURS

A 6-rib rib roast

2 tablespoons whole black peppercorns

¼ cup finely ground coffee

3 tablespoons thyme, finely chopped

2 tablespoons dark brown sugar

2 tablespoons fresh sea salt

2 teaspoons ground mustard

1 teaspoon smoked paprika

3 tablespoons extra-virgin olive oil

3 bunches fresh rosemary (optional)

A coffee based rub is nearly always paired with beef because of its bold, though soft flavors. The coffee rub is heavy, but it's very accessible because its flavors largely remain on the outside of the roast. Maybe, when applied to the rib roast the flavors will get into the cap of the roast, though for the most part, the finely ground coffee and split peppercorns will form a thick, charred crust on the outside of the roast.

1. Remove the rib roast from the refrigerator 1 hour before cooking and let stand at room temperature.

2. Preheat the oven to 450 degrees.

3. Place the whole black peppercorns in a small, sealable bag and seal tightly. Place the bag on a flat surface and then, using the bottom of a heavy pan such as a cast-iron skillet, firmly pound the peppercorns so that they split into large pieces. Ideally, you'll want the peppercorns to be much more coarse than what a traditional pepper mill will do. Remove the split peppercorns from the bag and add to a small bowl. Mix in the fresh sea salt.

4. Add the next 6 ingredients to the salt and peppercorns and combine so it forms an evenly-distributed rub.

5. Next, when the meat's temperature has lowered, generously apply the extra-virgin olive oil to the prime rib. Using your hands, apply the rub to the prime rib, making sure that all areas of the meat under the fat-cap also receive the rub. If you'd like to add a rosemary element to the prime rib, divide the bunches of rosemary evenly and place in between the ribs. Tie firmly with butcher's twine so the rosemary stays in place while roasting.

6. Transfer the coffee-rubbed prime rib to a large rack set in a roasting pan. Then transfer the pan to the oven and sear for about 15 minutes.

7. Reduce the heat to 325 degrees and cook for 2½ to 3 hours, until a thermometer registers 125 degrees for medium-rare. During the roasting process, the crust of the rib roast may begin to brown—if that is the case, gently cover the rib roast with a sheet of aluminum foil in order to help maintain the moisture on the cap of the roast.

8. Remove the rib roast from the oven, transfer to a large carving board, and let stand for about 10 minutes before carving, allowing it to properly store its juices and flavor.

AU JUS, SAUCES, AND GRAVIES

AU JUS, LITERALLY MEANING "WITH ITS OWN JUICES," IS THE CLASSIC ACCOMPANIMENT TO ALL PRIME RIB DINNERS. At its most basic form, au jus is a combination of the cooked proteins found in the muscles and fibers from the meat, along with the lipids from the blood. Since these "juices" of the meat come naturally with a slow-roasting technique (note that some sort of roasting pan is required to catch the juices), they serve as the most foundational element to any sauce or gravy that you prepare for your dinner. Because the earthy, natural flavors of a classic au jus are extremely compatible and accessible, they pair well with practically all elements of the dinner. No matter the occasion, an au jus should always be prepared just after removing the rib roast from the roasting pan. The flavors you aim for are entirely up to you—the technique remains the same.

To begin, remove the rib roast from the pan and strain the pan drippings through a fine sieve. Then, pass the strained juiced through a fat separator (a simple spoon will do). For more flavor, do not discard the browned bits that have remained on the bottom of the roasting pan. Add the juices to the roasting pan and set over medium-high heat; note that you may need to use two burners.

Now it's time to add fundamental elements to your au jus that will enhance its consistency and flavor. For a rib roast, you'll want to find a nice bottle of dry red wine—preferably the same one that you'll be serving with dinner—and add 1 cup of it to your roasting pan, along with a 2 cups of beef broth (note the 1:2 ratio here between the red wine and beef broth). Do not add a stock to your au jus; always a broth. A beef stock will actually have too much flavor and it will overpower your au jus.

With the roasting pan placed over medium-high heat, bring your juices to a boil and then reduce until you have about 1 to 1½ cups of au jus. Stir the au jus occasionally, scraping off the browned bits from the bottom so that they naturally are incorporated into the au jus.

Finally, you'll need to add seasonings to your au jus. Depending on the environment and mood of your dinner, you may want to pair the rib roast with the most natural form of au jus. If this is the case, you'll want to remove the roasting pan from the heat and season with the coarsely ground black pepper and fresh sea salt. However, if you want to add some additional natural ingredients to your au jus, consider a couple tablespoons of finely chopped fresh herbs such as thyme, rosemary, or flat-leaf parsley. If you want a little creaminess, whisk in 1 tablespoon of unsalted butter just before seasoning with the coarsely ground black pepper and fresh sea salt. Some chefs will even add soy sauce or Worcestershire sauce to the au jus at this final stage, and I encourage you to try that once in a while.

Although the classic au jus is most often imagined alongside a rib roast, it is essential to understand that an au jus can really be prepared with any slow-roasted meat, including poultry. For your convenience, I've prepared three basic ingredient lists for au jus, including one for poultry dishes, so that you can see the flexibility of an au jus and hopefully get an idea of where and how you'll want to experiment. Follow the three stages listed above and you'll have your very own au jus in no time at all.

A sauce or gravy is crucial not only to a great prime rib dinner but to any meat dish. From classics such as Fundamental Prime-Rib Gravy to Farm-Style Chimichurri, each sauce is rooted in a simple combination of flavors that's enhanced by softer flavors found in other ingredients. You want flavors that are bold but don't overpower the meat or sides. It's a creative balance.

With the recipes in this chapter, you'll discover there's a simple framework for making sauces and gravies. Add the right ingredients at the right times, and you'll have a sauce perfect for your prime rib dinner.

Sauces are structured with one of two foundational components: liquids or vegetables. Nearly all sauces that are liquids start with oil, cream, stock, broth, beer, wine, and liquor.

For prime rib sauces, we most often work with oil, cream, stock, broth, and wine because of their soft, yet heavy flavors. To begin, sauté compatible-flavored vegetables such as garlic, onion, or shallot in a skillet or saucepan and cook lightly, so their juices become a blanket to the pan. Next, add your liquid to the pan and bring to a strong simmer, and then start the reduction process. For most sauces, you'll want to reduce them by at least half. Depending on how strong you want your sauce to be, add herbs and other spices at some point during the reduction process. After reduction, serve the sauce immediately, or strain and then serve.

Sauces made from vegetables, such as a Chimichurri or Basil Pesto, don't take long to prepare, and they're compatible with a variety of meats. Ingredients for these sauces are typically either finely chopped and then combined in a small bowl with some extra-virgin olive oil, or pulsed in a food processor with the olive oil gradually beat in.

Gravy is a must-have when it comes to prime rib, and roux is a necessary component of gravy. A white roux is composed of equal parts butter and flour and can either be made ahead of time or added to the sauce toward the end of the cooking process. When making ahead, set a small frying pan over medium heat and add 1 or 2 tablespoons of unsalted butter to the pan. When it has melted, stir in an equal amount of flour and beat into the butter until the roux reaches a thick mixture. The roux should not be browned, though it should have a hint of gold. Add the white roux toward the end of the sauce's cooking and then continue to heat for another 1 to 2 minutes so the sauce thickens and becomes a gravy.

BASIC AU JUS

1 cup dry red wine • 2 cups beef broth • 1 tablespoon unsalted butter (optional) • Coarsely ground black pepper • Fresh sea salt

AU JUS WITH HERBS

1 cup dry red wine • 2 cups beef broth • 1 teaspoon fresh rosemary, finely chopped • 1 teaspoon fresh thyme, finely chopped • 1 teaspoon flat-leaf parsley, finely chopped • 1 teaspoon Worcestershire sauce (optional) • Coarsely ground black pepper • Fresh sea salt

 # POULTRY AU JUS

1 cup dry white wine • 2 cups chicken broth • 2 teaspoons flat-leaf parsley, finely chopped • 1 tablespoon unsalted butter • Coarsely ground black pepper • Fresh sea salt

FUNDAMENTAL PRIME-RIB GRAVY

MAKES 6 TO 8 SERVINGS
ACTIVE TIME: 20 MINUTES
TOTAL TIME: 30 MINUTES

1 cup dry red wine

1½ cups beef or veal stock or broth

1 tablespoon unsalted butter

1 tablespoon all-purpose flour

1 tablespoon fresh thyme, finely chopped

Coarsely ground black pepper

Fresh sea salt

The fundamental part to any gravy comes from the juices leftover in the pan after the rib roast has been cooked. Likewise, your gravy goes hand-in-hand with the roasting technique—it's essential that you use a technique that involves a roasting pan so that the juices from the prime rib slowly accumulate at the bottom of the pan.

A gravy is not too different from an au jus, other than that it adds a white roux to the cooking process.

1. When the roast is finished, remove it and the roasting rack from the pan and transfer to a large carving board. I recommend covering the roast with a sheet or two of aluminum foil so it stays warm. Pour the juices from the roasting pan into a fat separator; discard the fat and return the juices to the original roasting pan. Note that there is still flavor blanketing the roasting pan, so be sure to use the same pan.

2. Next, set the roasting pan over high heat—it may be necessary to use two burners if the roasting rack is too large for one. Add the red wine and stock or broth to the pan and bring to a light simmer, using a wooden spatula to scrape off any bits that still remain on the bottom of the pan so they are incorporated into the sauce.

3. Whisk the butter into the sauce, followed by the flour. Depending on how thick you want the gravy, add more butter and flour in incremental, equal proportions.

4. When thickened, about 1 to 2 minutes later, turn the heat off and stir in the thyme. Taste the gravy and season with the coarsely ground black pepper and fresh sea salt; then transfer to a small gravy boat. Serve hot.

TIP: IF YOU DON'T HAVE A HAVE FAT SEPARATOR, BRING THE ROASTING PAN TO THE SINK AND TILT TO ONE SIDE. NEXT, WITH A LARGE SPOON OR LADLE, SLOWLY SPOON AWAY THE FAT THAT REMAINS AT THE TOP OF THE DISH.

MADEIRA SAUCE

MAKES 6 SERVINGS
ACTIVE TIME: 20 MINUTES
TOTAL TIME: 25 MINUTES

2 tablespoons unsalted butter

1 small shallot, finely chopped

1 tablespoon all-purpose flour

¼ cup dry red wine

¾ cup Madeira

1 cup beef stock or broth, canned or purchased from local butcher

2 sprigs fresh thyme, leaves removed

2 sprigs fresh rosemary, leaves removed

Coarsely ground black pepper

Fresh sea salt

At the White Barn Inn in Kennebunk, Maine, where I worked for some time, we always paired a classic Madeira sauce with our beef tenderloin, served over whipped potatoes. A very condensed sauce, the most fundamental element to a Madeira is the beef stock. Fresh beef stock is always best. Chances are, your local butcher can give you either a fresh stock or the best instructions on how use their bones properly in your stock.

1. Add the butter to a medium cast-iron skillet and warm over medium heat. Then add the chopped shallot and sauté until translucent, about 4 minutes.

2. Add the flour to the pan and cook for 1 minute. Once incorporated, turn the heat to medium-low and then add the dry red wine, Madeira, beef stock or broth, thyme, and rosemary.

3. Cook until the sauce has been significantly reduced, to your desired consistency, about 15 to 20 minutes.

4. When the sauce is reduced, remove the skillet from the stovetop and season with the coarsely ground black pepper and fresh sea salt. Spoon the Madeira sauce over the cuts of rib roast.

VARIATION: IF YOU WANT A STRONGER MADEIRA SAUCE, ADD 1 TABLESPOON OF BEEF DEMI-GLACE TO THE SAUCE ALONG WITH THE BEEF STOCK. YOU CAN FIND BEEF DEMI-GLACE AT THE GROCERY STORE NEAR THE BEEF BROTHS AND STOCKS.

HOMEMADE KETCHUP

MAKES 6 TO 8 SERVINGS
ACTIVE TIME: 10 MINUTES
TOTAL TIME: 15 MINUTES

3 cups puréed tomatoes

¼ medium lemon, juiced

2 tablespoons extra-virgin olive oil

½ medium white onion, finely chopped

2 garlic cloves, minced

¼ cup dark brown sugar

½ cup apple cider vinegar

½ cup water

Coarsely ground black pepper

Fresh sea salt

You'll be surprised at just how well homemade ketchup pairs with a grilled prime rib, especially when used as a condiment for dipping. Most ketchup made by large-scale manufacturers is largely based in sucrose. Because of this, when we have natural, homemade ketchup, we tend to think of it as something entirely different than ketchup. Homemade ketchup should always be grounded in puréed tomatoes and vinegar rather than dark brown sugar.

1. In a medium bowl, combine the puréed tomatoes, lemon juice, extra-virgin olive oil, onion, garlic, and dark brown sugar. Let rest for 15 minutes.

2. Next, gradually whisk in the apple cider vinegar and water. Season with the coarsely ground black pepper and fresh sea salt.

3. You can serve your ketchup right away or let the flavors meld overnight in the refrigerator.

BASIL PESTO

MAKES 6 SERVINGS
ACTIVE TIME: 15 MINUTES
TOTAL TIME: 15 MINUTES

⅓ cup, plus 2 teaspoons extra-virgin olive oil

⅓ cup pine nuts

3 cups fresh basil leaves

¼ small shallot

2 garlic cloves

¼ cup Parmesan cheese, freshly grated

Coarsely ground black pepper

Fresh sea salt

Pesto is rooted in herbs and pine nuts—two of the most versatile flavors. It not only goes well when used as a sauce or crust to the rib roast, but it works even better when spooned into a Classic Baked Potato (page 160) with a charred crust. You've got to try it!

1. Add 2 teaspoons of the extra-virgin olive oil to a small frying pan and place on the stovetop over medium heat. When hot, add the pine nuts and toast for a minute or two until golden, not browned. Remove from the heat and transfer to a small cup.

2. In a small food processor, pulse the pine nuts, basil leaves, shallot, and garlic into a thick paste. Next, slowly incorporate the remaining extra-virgin olive oil into the pesto, until you reach your desired consistency.

3. Using a spatula, remove the pesto from the processor and place in a medium bowl. With a spoon, mix in the Parmesan cheese and then season with the coarsely ground black pepper and fresh sea salt. Serve at room temperature, or lightly chilled.

VARIATION: IF YOU WANT A COARSER PESTO (OR DON'T HAVE A FOOD PROCESSOR), YOU CAN ALWAYS USE A CHEF'S KNIFE AND CUTTING BOARD TO CHOP THE INGREDIENTS. IN A SMALL BOWL, COMBINE THEM, AND THEN LET THE PESTO MARINATE FOR 1 HOUR BEFORE SERVING.

PIZZAIOLA

MAKES 6 TO 8 SERVINGS
ACTIVE TIME: 35 MINUTES
TOTAL TIME: 45 MINUTES

¼ cup extra-virgin olive oil

4 garlic cloves, finely chopped

2 pounds plum tomatoes, crushed by hand

¼ cup sun-dried tomatoes

1 sprig fresh oregano

1 sprig fresh thyme

1 teaspoon red pepper flakes (optional)

¼ cup dry white wine

½ cup fresh basil leaves, finely chopped

Coarsely ground black pepper

Fresh sea salt

I first had a version of this dish at the Palm in New York City. My father and I ordered two New York Strips and then, rather unexpectedly, a side of spicy marinara, just slightly less complex than a pizzaiola sauce. With the beef and pizzaiola combined, the flavors were simply breathtaking—spicy though sweet; rich yet light. Weeks later, I tried this pizzaiola sauce with a rotisseried rib roast and the flavors exploded—there's really nothing quite like a pizzaiola!

1. Add the extra-virgin olive oil to a cast-iron skillet and place over medium heat. When the oil is hot, add the garlic and cook until golden, about 1 to 2 minutes.

2. Next, add the plum tomatoes, sun-dried tomatoes, oregano, thyme, and red pepper flakes if using. Simmer for 15 minutes, and then add the wine and basil and season with pepper and salt.

3. Simmer for 20 more minutes, then remove the skillet from the stovetop and serve warm.

SUN-DRIED TOMATO PESTO

MAKES 6 TO 8 SERVINGS
ACTIVE TIME: 10 MINUTES
TOTAL TIME: 10 MINUTES

12 sun-dried tomatoes

½ cup fresh basil leaves

¼ small shallot

¼ cup pine nuts

1 garlic clove

1 tablespoon coarsely ground black pepper

1 teaspoon fresh sea salt

½ cup extra-virgin olive oil

This is such an easy recipe to make—all you need is a food processor, or just a chef's knife, a carving board, and a small bowl to hold everything! I recommend serving the sun-dried tomato pesto in the summertime with a grilled prime rib—I'd even rub a little of the pesto on the ends of the rib roast toward the end of the grilling process!

1. In a small food processor, combine all the ingredients except the extra-virgin olive oil and pulse into a thick mixture.

2. Slowly add the extra-virgin olive oil and process until reaching your desired consistency. Serve at room temperature or lightly chilled.

VARIATION: IF YOU WANT A COARSER PESTO (OR DON'T HAVE A FOOD PROCESSOR), YOU CAN ALWAYS USE A CHEF'S KNIFE AND CUTTING BOARD TO CHOP THE INGREDIENTS. IN A SMALL BOWL, COMBINE THEM, AND THEN LET THE PESTO MARINATE FOR 1 HOUR BEFORE SERVING.

GARLIC & CHIVE STEAK SAUCE

MAKES 6 SERVINGS
ACTIVE TIME: 10 MINUTES
TOTAL TIME: 15 MINUTES

½ cup sour cream

¼ cup chives, finely chopped

3 garlic cloves, minced

¼ small lemon, juiced

Coarsely ground black pepper

Fresh sea salt

The flavor of chives is very similar to that of a mild onion. Sauces rooted in simple flavors such as garlic and chives always go well with red meat and potato side dishes.

In a small bowl, whisk together the sour cream, chives, garlic, and lemon juice, and then season with the coarsely ground black pepper.

TIP: STORE IN THE REFRIGERATOR FOR UP TO 3 DAYS, AND SERVE AT ROOM TEMPERATURE.

FARM-STYLE CHIMICHURRI

Courtesy of Marin Sun Farms
Point Reyes Station, CA

MAKES 6 SERVINGS
ACTIVE TIME: 10 MINUTES
TOTAL TIME: 15 MINUTES

2 bunches fresh parsley

1 bunch fresh oregano

1 bunch fresh thyme

2 lemons, juiced

1 shallot, minced

2 tablespoons sherry vinegar

¼ cup capers, rinsed and roughly chopped

½ cup extra-virgin olive oil

Coarsely ground black pepper

Fresh sea salt

Using a food processor, pulse all ingredients to desired consistency. It's as simple as that!

SALSA VERDE

MAKES 4 TO 6 SERVINGS
ACTIVE TIME: 20 MINUTES
TOTAL TIME: 45 MINUTES

10 tomatillos

1 small red onion, cut in half

2 tablespoons extra-virgin olive oil

Coarsely ground black pepper

Fresh sea salt

1 bunch fresh cilantro leaves, chopped

2 cloves garlic, chopped

1 teaspoon cumin

Courtesy of Erik Diamond of Quail Hill Farm · Amagansett, NY

1. Turn the broiler on.

2. Toss the tomatillos and red onion in the extra-virgin olive oil, coarsely ground black pepper, and fresh sea salt to coat.

3. Place tomatillo mixture in a pan and broil until slightly charred. Transfer mixture to a blender with pan juices, cilantro, and garlic, and blend until smooth. Add cumin and adjust seasonings.

CHILE OIL

MAKES 6 TO 8 SERVINGS
ACTIVE TIME: 10 MINUTES
TOTAL TIME: 30 MINUTES

1 cup extra-virgin olive oil

3 tablespoons chile flakes

Coarsely ground black pepper

Olive oils are infused when placed over medium-low heat and "cooked" for about 3 minutes. With the Rosemary-Infused Olive Oil (page 155), there's no need to bring the oil to a simmer because the flavors from the rosemary infuse easily. However, with Chile Oil, it's necessary for the oil to reach a simmer because the spice from the chile flakes is condensed and not transmitted without heat. When finished, spoon the sauce alongside the prime rib and on the skin of a whole Classic Baked Potato (page 162).

1. Place the olive oil, chile flakes, and a pinch of coarsely ground black pepper in a small saucepan and set over medium-low heat. Bring the oil to a simmer and let cook for 3 minutes. Turn off the heat and let rest for 30 minutes until it returns to room temperature.

2. If you'd like, strain the oil through a fine sieve or serve as is.

MERLOT GRAVY

MAKES 6 TO 8 SERVINGS
ACTIVE TIME: 45 MINUTES
TOTAL TIME: 1 HOUR AND 15 MINUTES

3 cups Merlot

1 cup chicken broth

1 cup beef broth

1 tablespoon extra-virgin olive oil

1 medium shallot, finely chopped

2 garlic cloves, minced

2 tablespoons flat-leaf parsley, finely chopped

2 tablespoons unsalted butter

2 tablespoons all-purpose flour

Coarsely ground black pepper

Fresh sea salt

Merlot is a traditional wine that normally falls in the middle of red wines: not too fruity, neither too earthy. Because of its compatible flavors, Merlot works very well with meat dishes, and especially gravies. A gravy and its pairing with a prime rib dinner can really make all the difference, so I encourage you to use a nice bottle of Merlot that you will also drink with your meal—see recommendations on pages 68 to 75.

1. Remove the roast and the roasting rack from the pan and transfer to a large carving board. I recommend covering the roast with a sheet or two of aluminum foil so that it stays warm. Pour the juices from the roasting pan into a fat separator; discard the fat and return the juices to the original roasting pan. Note that there is still flavor blanketing the roasting pan, so be sure to use the same pan.

2. Add the Merlot, chicken broth, and beef broth to the roasting pan and set over medium heat. Because of the size of the typical roasting pan, you will most likely need to use two burners for this. Use a wooden spatula to scrape the bits from the rib roast off the bottom of the roasting pan. Let the wine and broths simmer for 30 to 45 minutes, until it has reduced by half.

3. When your sauce is just about finished reducing, add the extra-virgin olive oil to a medium saucepan and place over medium heat. When hot, add the shallot and sauté for about 3 to 4 minutes, until it's translucent. Next, add the garlic and cook for about 2 minutes, until golden, not browned. Then, pour the sauce from the roasting pan into the saucepan, and stir thoroughly.

4. Add the unsalted butter to the saucepan, followed by the flour and parsley. Reduce the heat to medium-low, and let simmer for 5 to 10 minutes, until the sauce has reached a thickened consistency. Remove from the heat and season with the coarsely ground black pepper and fresh sea salt. Serve hot.

MUSHROOM CREAM SAUCE

MAKES 6 SERVINGS
ACTIVE TIME: 25 MINUTES
TOTAL TIME: 30 MINUTES

1 tablespoon unsalted butter

1 small shallot, minced

2 garlic cloves, minced

2 to 3 cups white button mushrooms, halved and sliced

¾ cup heavy whipping cream

1 tablespoon fresh thyme, finely chopped

Coarsely ground black pepper

Fresh sea salt

Mushrooms have a very heavy, hearty flavor that's perfect when sautéed and braised with a cream base, as seen here. Ladle the mushrooms and sauce over a freshly cut prime rib.

1. Add the unsalted butter to a medium cast-iron skillet and set over medium heat. When melted, add the shallot and cook until translucent, about 3 to 4 minutes. Add the garlic and sauté until browned, about 2 more minutes.

2. Next, add the mushrooms to the skillet and cook until lightly browned, about 4 to 6 minutes. Then, stir in the heavy whipping cream and thyme. Bring the cream to a boil and then reduce the heat to low and cook for about 10 minutes, until the cream has reduced and the mushrooms are tender.

3. Remove the pan from the heat and season with the coarsely ground black pepper and fresh sea salt. Serve immediately.

ROSEMARY-INFUSED OLIVE OIL

MAKES 6 TO 8 SERVINGS
ACTIVE TIME: 15 MINUTES
TOTAL TIME: 20 MINUTES

6 large sprigs fresh rosemary

1 cup extra-virgin olive oil

Coarsely ground black pepper

Fresh sea salt

The soft rosemary flavors always go well around with a rib roast and its sides. It's extremely simple to infuse olive oil, and I usually double this recipe so that when I prepare my rib roast I'll rub it with the rosemary-infused olive oil. I especially love serving this infused olive oil with Cheese, Herb & Garlic Bread (page 213).

1. In a small saucepan, combine the rosemary and extra-virgin olive oil and place on the stovetop with the heat off. Set the heat to medium-low and let the olive oil heat, but do not let it reach a boil. When hot, turn the heat off and let the rosemary infuse into the olive oil for 1 to 2 hours.

2. Strain the oil into a jar and keep at room temperature or in the refrigerator. Store for 2 or 4 months, respectively.

HERBED BUTTER

MAKES 6 SERVINGS
ACTIVE TIME: 10 MINUTES
TOTAL TIME: 15 MINUTES

1 tablespoon fresh rosemary leaves

1 tablespoon fresh thyme leaves

1 tablespoon fresh chives

1 tablespoon flat-leaf parsley leaves

½ medium garlic clove

½ cup (1 stick) unsalted butter, room temperature

1 teaspoon coarsely ground black pepper

1 teaspoon fresh sea salt

Herbed butter is a staple with any prime rib dish. Place a little on a Classic Baked Potato (page 160), a fresh filet of rib roast, or a warm Country Roll (page 218). You can make this dish up to four days in advance, just be sure to cover and refrigerate it immediately after pulsing in the food processor.

1. In a small food processor, pulse the rosemary, thyme, chives, parsley, and garlic, followed by the butter. Season with the coarsely ground black pepper and fresh sea salt, and then cover and transfer to the refrigerator for up to 4 days.

TIP: BEFORE SERVING, REMOVE THE HERBED BUTTER FROM THE REFRIGERATOR AND BRING TO ROOM TEMPERATURE BY LETTING IT STAND FOR 1 HOUR.

SIDES

LARGELY BASED UPON THEIR SIMPLICITY AND NATURAL FLAVORS, SIDE DISHES ARE ALWAYS ESSENTIAL TO ANY DINNER. Personally, I prefer to always have my sides be rooted in produce with just a few additional elements, if any—maybe just a pinch of coarsely ground black pepper and fresh sea salt, and a splash of extra-virgin olive oil. Most of the time, cooking times are always much quicker than the time to takes to cook a full rib roast, so be sure to time these sides so that they come out just in time for the dinner—if you overshoot either the side or the prime rib, simply cover the dish with a sheet of aluminum foil and set in a warm place.

For most of my sides, such as baked potatoes and asparagus, I prefer them to be slightly charred. Usually I turn to my broiler for this. The broiler, or the upper heat source in your oven, reaches an extremely-hot temperature and cooks your ingredients very quickly, though because the heat is very high, it mostly cooks on the outside, encouraging a perfect char to your vegetable. To get an even better char, rub a half-teaspoon of extra-virgin olive oil onto whatever vegetable you are cooking and you'll be surprised to find that the char is more even and crisp!

Always use your broiler carefully—and I mean always! One time, after a long summer day, my father and I went down to the store and picked up a couple steaks and potatoes to make a quick dinner on the grill. He was in charge of the steaks, I on the potatoes. After baking them for about 30 to 40 minutes, I decided to position the rack to the upper-portion of the oven and then switched on the broiler. While fixing my father and I two gin and tonics, just six minutes later, smoke and flames were bursting inside the oven and, what should happen but the potatoes were toast—literally! Although we ate our two steaks unaccompanied by any vegetables, we both learned that the broiler is definitely not your slow cooker. It needs tending to and careful attention.

CLASSIC BAKED POTATO

MAKES 6 SERVINGS
ACTIVE TIME: 10 MINUTES
TOTAL TIME: 50 MINUTES

6 russet potatoes, washed and scrubbed

2 tablespoons extra-virgin olive oil

Coarsely ground black pepper

Fresh sea salt

¼ cup chopped fresh chives (optional, for toppings)

¼ cup sour cream (optional, for toppings)

¼ cup aged Parmesan cheese (optional, for toppings)

½ cup (1 stick) unsalted butter, softened (optional, for toppings)

Bacon pieces (optional)

The baked potato is a staple of all prime rib dinners. To make these even better than they already are, there's not much more you need besides some chopped chives or a spoonful of sour cream. In my opinion, the skin of the potato is the most flavorful part and should be treated with the most care—sometimes I'll even broil them for a minute or two at the end just so those skins get a little charred!

1. Preheat the oven to 400 degrees, placing the rack in the center of the oven.

2. While the oven heats, pierce your russet potatoes with a fork and then rub lightly with the extra-virgin olive oil. Season the potatoes generously with the coarsely ground black pepper and fresh sea salt.

3. Place the potatoes directly on the oven rack and bake for about 45 minutes, until the skins are crisp and the potatoes can be easily pierced with a fork.

4. Remove the potatoes from the oven and serve immediately along with any of the optional toppings listed.

CHARRED SWEET POTATOES

MAKES 4 SERVINGS
ACTIVE TIME: 30 MINUTES
TOTAL TIME: ABOUT 1 HOUR

4 large sweet potatoes

2 tablespoons extra-virgin olive oil

Coarsely ground black pepper

Fresh sea salt

Butter for serving

Though they're most often simply baked, sweet potatoes taste even better and more flavorful when baked, and then broiled and charred. On a summer evening when you may want more of a smoky flavor, consider grilling the sweet potatoes. Throw some pre-soaked maple woodchips over the coals and grill with the lid closed.

1. Preheat the oven to 350 degrees, placing the rack in the upper-middle position.

2. Brush the sweet potatoes lightly with the extra-virgin olive oil and then season with the coarsely ground black pepper and sea salt.

3. Place the sweet potatoes in a glass-baking dish. Transfer to oven, and bake for 50 minutes, turning every 15 minutes.

4. When a fork can pierce the sweet potatoes fairly easily, turn on the broiler and cook for about 5 more minutes, until the skins are charred. Stand by the oven and watch the potatoes closely, making sure that the broiler doesn't set them aflame!

5. Remove from the oven and let cool for 4 minutes before serving with butter.

BOURBON-BRAISED CHESTNUT AND ONION CONFIT

Courtesy of Glynwood · Cold Spring, NY

MAKES 4 SERVINGS
ACTIVE TIME: 25 MINUTES
TOTAL TIME: 40 MINUTES

1 pound cipollini onions

6 tablespoons (¾ stick) salted butter

2 large shallots, minced

2 cups chestnuts, roasted, shelled, and skinned, half chopped and half remaining whole

¾ to 1 cup bourbon

Coarsely ground black pepper

Fresh sea salt

1. Blanche onions in a large saucepan of boiling water for 3 minutes, then drain and transfer to a bowl of ice water. Peel the onions, taking care to not take too many layers of the onion with the peel. Slice larger onions in half crosswise.

2. In a large sauté pan or cast-iron skillet over medium heat, add 4 tablespoons of the butter. Add the shallots and sauté until lightly browned. Add the onions and continue to sauté for approximately 10 minutes, until the edges begin to caramelize.

3. Add the chestnuts and remaining butter and toss with the onions and shallots. Continue to cook until chestnuts have started to brown slightly.

4. Turn heat up to high and add the bourbon. Toss and simmer until most of the liquid has evaporated. Season with the coarsely ground black pepper and fresh sea salt. Serve warm.

TIP: WHILE YOU'VE GOT THE BOURBON OUT, YOU MIGHT AS WELL POUR SOME ON THE ROCKS.

BRAISED VIDALIA ONIONS & MUSHROOMS

MAKES 6 SERVINGS
ACTIVE TIME: 15 MINUTES
TOTAL TIME: 20 MINUTES

3 tablespoons extra-virgin olive oil

1 large Vidalia onion, peeled and chopped into ¼-inch slices

1 pint Portobello mushrooms, sliced

Fresh sea salt

Coarsely ground black pepper

The best way to write about Braised Vidalia Onions & Mushrooms is to describe it as a dish with character and soul. When raw, Vidalia onions have a slightly sharp flavor, while the mushrooms can be stiff on their own. However when you take a cast-iron skillet and braise the onions and mushrooms, the two opposite flavors find a deep, common ground. Be sure to season generously!

1. Heat the extra-virgin olive oil in a medium cast-iron skillet over low-medium heat.

2. When hot, add the Vidalia onions and Portobello mushrooms to the skillet and cook until tender, about 10 to 15 minutes.

3. Remove the skillet from the heat, season the onions and mushrooms with salt and pepper, and serve immediately.

FINGERLING POTATOES WITH HERBS

MAKES 6 TO 8 SERVINGS
ACTIVE TIME: 15 MINUTES
TOTAL TIME: 40 MINUTES

4 pounds fingerling potatoes, halved lengthwise

2 tablespoons extra-virgin olive oil

2 tablespoons fresh rosemary, finely chopped

2 tablespoons fresh thyme, finely chopped

Coarsely ground black pepper

Fresh sea salt

This dish goes well with practically every meal. Usually, I'll have lots of prime rib left over from the night before, and I'll slice up several strips of prime rib and use it on top of egg-and-cheese sandwiches, served alongside some fingerling potatoes. Yum!

1. Preheat the oven to 400 degrees, placing the rack in the center of the oven.

2. In a large bowl, toss the fingerling potatoes with the extra-virgin olive oil, rosemary, and thyme, and then season generously with the coarsely ground black pepper and fresh sea salt.

3. Spread the fingerling potatoes evenly across a large baking sheet and transfer to the oven. Bake for 30 to 35 minutes, until the potatoes are browned and can be easily pierced with a fork.

4. Remove from the oven and serve immediately.

MASHED POTATOES

MAKES 6 SERVINGS

ACTIVE TIME: 30 MINUTES

TOTAL TIME: 45 MINUTES

3 pounds Yukon Gold potatoes, peeled and cut into quarters

1 cup half-and-half

½ cup (1 stick) unsalted butter, softened

Coarsely ground black pepper

Fresh sea salt

In my mind, the prime rib dinner always boils down to what I want to serve it with: baked or mashed potatoes. More often than not, I'll go with mashed potatoes. Making the perfect mashed potatoes is an art; it takes just the right potatoes, the proper cooking time, and the perfect blend of cream and butter. Always take your time when mashing the potatoes, tasting as you go along, until you've arrived at your desired consistency.

1. Place the potatoes in a large stockpot and fill with water so that it covers the potatoes by 1 inch.

2. Place the stockpot on the stove and bring to a boil. Cook for about 20 minutes, until you can pierce the potatoes with a fork. Remove from the pot from the heat and drain the water, leaving the potatoes in it.

3. Using a potato masher or fork (a little more work, but still a masher nonetheless), start mashing the potatoes so they break apart. Gradually beat in the half-and-half and butter, tasting the potatoes as you go along, until you arrive at the perfect blend of creamy, buttery, mashed potatoes. Season with the coarsely ground black pepper and fresh sea salt, and then serve warm.

BAKED ASPARAGUS

MAKES 4 SERVINGS
ACTIVE TIME: 10 MINUTES
TOTAL TIME: 30 MINUTES

1 to 1½ pounds fresh asparagus, washed and scrubbed

3 tablespoons extra-virgin olive oil

Coarsely ground black pepper

Fresh sea salt

¼ cup aged Parmesan

Often considered the ultimate side, baked asparagus works well with virtually any dish.

1. Preheat the oven to 425 degrees.

2. Place the asparagus in a glass baking dish. Drizzle the extra-virgin olive oil over the asparagus, rolling them around with a fork so that all sides receive equal amounts of olive oil. Then season with the coarsely ground black pepper and fresh sea salt.

3. Transfer the asparagus to the oven and roast until browned and tender, about 15 minutes.

4. Remove the baking dish from the oven and let rest for 5 minutes before serving. When plated, season each helping of asparagus with the Parmesan cheese.

VARIATION: CONSIDER WRAPPING BUNDLES OF THREE ASPARAGUS WITH A THICK PIECE OF BACON, AND THEN SAUTÉING UNTIL THE BACON IS CRISP.

BONE MARROW MASHED POTATOES

GLUTEN GF FREE

MAKES 6 TO 8 SERVINGS
ACTIVE TIME: 25 MINUTES
TOTAL TIME: 1 HOUR

8 Yukon Gold potatoes, peeled and cut into quarters

4 to 6 large beef marrow bones, halved lengthwise

½ cup half-and-half

½ cup (1 stick) unsalted butter, softened

1 teaspoon fresh rosemary, finely chopped

Coarsely ground black pepper

Fresh sea salt

The first time I had these was at the Union Square Cafe in New York City. Served alongside a charred rib eye for two, the Bone Marrow Mashed Potatoes stole the show. Roasted bone marrow goes extremely well as a spread to smear across toasted breads because of its natural, buttery flavors. Likewise, it goes even better when mixed into some mashed potatoes. Be sure to spoon some hot au jus onto the potatoes just before serving.

1. Preheat the oven to 375 degrees, placing the rack in the center of the oven.

2. Place the marrow bones on a baking sheet, transfer to the oven, and then cook for about 15 minutes, until the marrow is nicely browned. Remove from the oven and let stand.

3. While the marrow bones are roasting, place the potatoes in a large stockpot and fill with water so that it covers the potatoes by 1 inch.

4. Place the stockpot on the stove and bring to a boil. Cook the potatoes by boiling for about 20 minutes, until you can pierce the potatoes with a fork. Remove the pot from heat and drain the water, leaving the potatoes in it.

5. Using a potato masher or fork, start mashing the potatoes so they begin to break apart. Gradually mash in the half-and-half and butter, tasting the potatoes as you go along, until arrive at the perfect blend of creamy, buttery, mashed potatoes.

6. Scoop the marrow from the bones and add to the potatoes, along with the rosemary. Mix thoroughly, and then season with the coarsely ground black pepper and fresh sea salt. Serve warm with hot au jus (page 131).

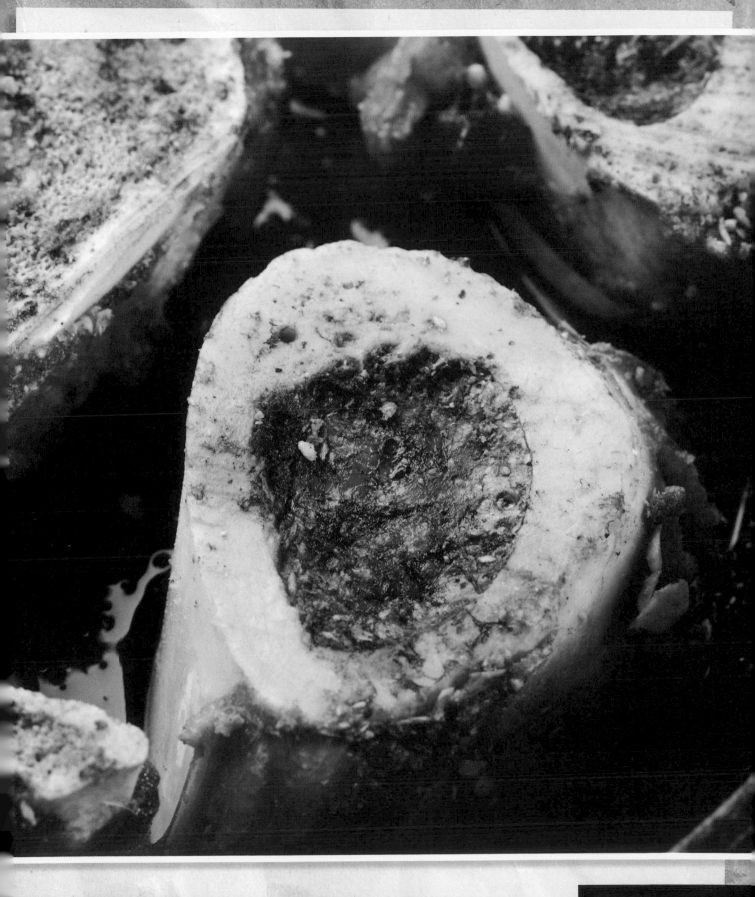

MARINATED GRILLED BUTTERNUT
WITH GARLIC-LEMON RICOTTA SPREAD

Courtesy of Chef Chrysa Robertson of McClendon's Select · Peoria, AZ

MAKES 6 SERVINGS
ACTIVE TIME: 20 MINUTES
TOTAL TIME: 2 TO 8 HOURS

1 medium-large butternut squash

3 tablespoons extra-virgin olive oil

2 tablespoons red wine vinegar

1 tablespoon honey

1 teaspoon fresh rosemary, chopped

2 cloves garlic, chopped

Coarsely ground black pepper

Fresh sea salt

GARLIC-LEMON RICOTTA SPREAD

2 cups fresh ricotta

Roasted garlic to taste

Lemon zest and juice to taste

Extra-virgin olive oil to taste

Fresh parsley, marjoram, thyme, chives, etc., finely chopped to taste

Coarsely ground black pepper

Fresh sea salt

1. Prepare a gas or charcoal grill to medium heat.

2. Peel and seed the butternut squash, and then cut into ½-inch thick slices. Set aside.

3. In a large bowl, combine the extra-virgin olive oil, red wine vinegar, honey, rosemary, and garlic, and toss with the sliced squash. Let marinate for 2 to 8 hours.

4. Season with the coarsely ground black pepper and fresh sea salt, and grill until tender, turning frequently.

5. Place the fresh ricotta in a medium bowl. Add remaining ingredients and stir to combine.

6. Serve the ricotta spread over toasted bread and top with the marinated grilled butternut squash.

ROASTED SEASONAL ROOT VEGETABLES

MAKES 6 SERVINGS
ACTIVE TIME: 20 MINUTES
TOTAL TIME: 50 MINUTES

2 pounds of mixed seasonal root vegetables (such as squash, rutabagas, beets, turnips, carrots, Jerusalem artichokes, yams, and potatoes), cubed to uniform ½-inch cubes

¼ cup fresh thyme, finely chopped

Lemon zest from 1 lemon

¼ cup extra-virgin olive oil

Coarsely ground black pepper to taste

Fresh sea salt to taste

Handful fresh parsley, finely chopped

Courtesy of AnnaRae Grabstein, Marin Sun Farms · Point Reyes Station, CA

1. Preheat the oven to 350 degrees.

2. In a large bowl, toss all the ingredients together, except the parsley.

3. Spread the vegetable mixture evenly on a baking sheet and roast until everything is cooked and crispy, but not brown.

4. Remove from the oven and sprinkle the finely chopped fresh parsley to finish.

STEWED BABY CARROTS

MAKES 6 SERVINGS
ACTIVE TIME: 15 MINUTES
TOTAL TIME: 20 MINUTES

1½ pounds fresh baby carrots

3 tablespoons unsalted butter

¼ cup brown sugar

Coarsely ground black pepper

Fresh sea salt

Sweet and hearty, stewed baby carrots are perfect when served alongside a potato- or grain-based side. Because of the recipe's simplicity, my mom always whips these up right before serving her prime rib on Christmas Eve.

1. In a small saucepan, add the carrots and fill with water—about 1 cup—so that it covers the carrots by 1 inch. Bring the water to a boil, then reduce to a simmer and cook for 8 to 10 minutes. Drain and place back on the stove at low-heat.

2. Add the butter and brown sugar to the pan; they will form a thick glaze. Continue to cook the carrots in the glaze on low heat, until they are tender and nicely coated with the glaze.

3. Remove from the heat and transfer carrots and glaze to a small bowl. Season with the coarsely ground black pepper and fresh sea salt, and serve warm.

SKILLET-SEARED CARROTS OVER YOGURT

Courtesy of Quail Hill Farm Amagansett, NY

MAKES 4 TO 5 SERVINGS
ACTIVE TIME: 20 MINUTES
TOTAL TIME: 40 MINUTES

¼ cup extra-virgin olive oil

12 thin carrots, washed and dried, but not peeled, unless they're very dirty

Coarsely ground black pepper

Fresh sea salt

¼ cup plain Greek yogurt, 2 percent or whole milk

Handful of fresh thyme leaves, finely chopped

Handful of flat-leaf parsley leaves, finely chopped

Honey (local honey, if possible)

1. Heat the extra-virgin olive oil in a cast-iron skillet large enough to hold the carrots in one layer. When it's very hot but not smoking, add the carrots, and season with coarsely ground black pepper and fresh sea salt. Move them around the pan until they are golden and soft, about 10 minutes.

2. In the meantime, smear the yogurt across a serving plate. When the carrots are cooked, place them on top of the yogurt. Top with the chopped herbs and drizzle with honey.

WHITE BEANS & DICED TOMATOES

MAKES 6 SERVINGS

ACTIVE TIME: 15 MINUTES

TOTAL TIME: 15 MINUTES

2 15-ounce cans cannellini beans, washed

1 pint cherry tomatoes, halved

½ cup fresh basil leaves, coarsely chopped

¼ cup flat-leaf parsley

3 tablespoons extra-virgin olive oil

½ medium lemon, juiced

2 garlic cloves, minced

1 tablespoon balsamic vinegar

¼ cup freshly grated Parmesan cheese

Coarsely ground black pepper

Fresh sea salt

For this recipe it's essential that you go to your local farmers' market to get the freshest ingredients. I especially love this dish when the tomatoes are slightly chilled and it's served on a warm summer afternoon mixed together with some leftover prime rib.

1. In a large bowl, mix together the cannellini beans, tomatoes, basil, and parsley. Transfer to the refrigerator.

2. In a small cup, whisk together the extra-virgin olive oil, lemon juice, garlic, and balsamic vinegar. Set aside.

3. Remove the cannellini beans and tomatoes from the refrigerator, and then toss with the balsamic vinegar. Top with the freshly grated Parmesan cheese, and season with the coarsely ground black pepper and fresh sea salt before serving.

SKILLET-SEARED GREEN BEAN CASSEROLE

MAKES 6 SERVINGS
ACTIVE TIME: 30 MINUTES
TOTAL TIME: 40 MINUTES

6 slices thick bacon

1 large shallot, finely chopped

2 pounds green beans, ends trimmed

2 tablespoons unsalted butter

2 garlic cloves, finely chopped

½ cup breadcrumbs

¼ cup freshly grated Parmesan cheese

Coarsely ground black pepper

Fresh sea salt

For my green bean casserole, I tread toward the lighter side with the bread-crumbs. To keep those natural flavors of the green beans, I recommend browning them in a cast-iron skillet before adding the breadcrumbs at the tail end of the searing.

1. Place a large cast-iron skillet on the stove over low-medium heat. When hot, add the bacon and shallots and cook until the bacon is crisp and the shallots are translucent, about 6 to 8 minutes. Transfer to a rack lined with paper towels.

2. Increase the heat to medium. Some of the oils from the bacon should remain in the bottom of the skillet. Add the green beans and sear until lightly browned, about 6 minutes. Add the bacon and shallots and toss well. Remove from the skillet and transfer to a large bowl.

3. In the same skillet, add the butter, followed by the garlic. Sear about 2 minutes, until the garlic is golden brown, and then remove from the heat. While the pan is still hot, stir in the breadcrumbs and sear lightly so that they absorb the flavors from the pan.

4. Pour the breadcrumbs from the pan onto the green beans and toss so they are evenly distributed. Garnish with the Parmesan cheese, and then season with the coarsely ground black pepper and fresh sea salt. Serve warm.

ITALIAN-STYLE BROCCOLI RAAB

Courtesy of Migliorelli Farm · Tivoli, NY

MAKES 4 TO 5 SERVINGS
ACTIVE TIME: 20 MINUTES
TOTAL TIME: 35 MINUTES

1 to 2 bunches fresh broccoli raab

2 to 3 tablespoons extra-virgin olive oil

2 to 3 cloves garlic, chopped

Coarsely ground black pepper

Fresh sea salt

1. Soak the broccoli raab in water. Coat the bottom of a pot with a generous amount of olive oil and then add the garlic. Sauté until just golden and then add the wet broccoli raab.

2. Add a pinch of coarsely ground black pepper and fresh sea salt and cover the pot. Let it cook for 20 to 30 minutes, until the broccoli raab is soft. It should never be al dente (undercooked). Serve immediately.

SAUTÉED KALE WITH PROSCIUTTO

MAKES 5 TO 6 SERVINGS
ACTIVE TIME: 15 MINUTES
TOTAL TIME: 30 MINUTES

8 to 10 slices prosciutto

2 tablespoons extra-virgin olive oil

2 garlic cloves, minced

2 pounds kale, coarsely chopped

2 tablespoons red wine vinegar

Coarsely ground black pepper

Fresh sea salt

You can boil, bake, and steam kale, but I prefer to sauté it with some olive oil and minced garlic so it develops soft flavors. Sautéing the kale not only cooks it quickly but also prevents the kale from wilting and losing its stiff texture.

1. Preheat the oven to 375 degrees.

2. Lay the prosciutto evenly on a baking sheet. Transfer the baking sheet to the oven and cook until the prosciutto is browned and crisp, about 15 minutes. Remove from the oven and place the prosciutto on a plate lined with paper towels. When cool, chop the prosciutto into medium-sized pieces.

3. Add the extra-virgin olive oil into a sauté pan with a lid and place over medium-high heat.

4. When hot, add the garlic and cook for about 2 minutes, until golden, not browned. Add the chopped kale and sauté, covered, for 7 minutes until softened.

5. Remove the lid and cook for 2 more minutes. Add the prosciutto and red wine vinegar and then remove from the heat. Season with ground black pepper and fresh sea salt, and serve warm.

BRUSSELS SPROUTS WITH CHARRED BACON

MAKES 6 SERVINGS
ACTIVE TIME: 20 MINUTES
TOTAL TIME: 45 MINUTES

6 strips thick bacon

2 tablespoons unsalted butter

1 medium shallot, coarsely chopped

1½ pounds Brussels sprouts

Coarsely ground black pepper

Fresh sea salt

Brussels sprouts with charred bacon is my favorite side. At Burger & Barrel in New York City, Executive Chef Josh Capon sautés his Brussels sprouts long enough at high heat so that their outer-most skins became a crisp shell. The oils from the shallot mix so well with the butter, and together they glaze over the Brussels sprouts and bacon.

1. Preheat the oven to 375 degrees, placing the rack in the upper-middle position.

2. In a large cast-iron skillet, place the bacon strips evenly across its surface. Transfer the skillet to the oven and cook until the bacon is brown and crisp, about 15 minutes.

3. Remove the skillet from the oven and place the bacon strips on sheets of paper towels. Be sure to leave the oil in the skillet. When cool, chop the bacon into medium-sized bits.

4. Heat the cast-iron skillet over high heat. When hot, melt the butter in the skillet and then add the shallot. Cook about 4 minutes, until translucent.

5. Next, add the Brussels sprouts to the skillet and cook for about 10 minutes, until browned. Stir in the bacon bits and warm for another 1 to 2 minutes. Remove the skillet from the heat and transfer the Brussels sprouts to a large bowl. Season with coarsely ground black pepper and fresh sea salt and serve warm.

CREAMED SPINACH

MAKES 4 SERVINGS
ACTIVE TIME: 15 MINUTES
TOTAL TIME: 20 MINUTES

1 tablespoon unsalted butter

1 small shallot, diced

2 garlic cloves, minced

2 pounds baby spinach, stems trimmed

⅓ cup heavy cream

Coarsely ground black pepper

Fresh sea salt

The key to a perfect dish of creamed spinach lays in the cream. Unlike most other creamed spinach recipes, this calls for just ⅓ cup of heavy cream. I prefer heavy cream over milk because you don't need as much of it, and the cream stews with the spinach as it's cooked in the seasoned cast-iron skillet.

1. Place the butter in a large cast-iron skillet on the stove over medium heat. When hot, add the diced shallot and garlic, and cook 3 to 4 minutes, until the garlic is golden and the shallot is translucent.

2. Add the spinach to the skillet in batches and cook until the spinach is warmed through. Pour in the heavy cream and cook for 6 to 8 minutes, until the liquid has reduced and the mixture has thickened.

3. Remove from the heat and then season with the coarsely ground black pepper and fresh sea salt. Serve warm.

SLOW-ROASTED ARTICHOKES

MAKES 6 SERVINGS
ACTIVE TIME: 20 MINUTES
TOTAL TIME: 50 MINUTES

4 large artichokes, stemmed

¼ cup extra-virgin olive oil

4 garlic cloves, minced

1 medium lemon, halved and juiced

Coarsely ground black pepper

Fresh sea salt

Rosemary for garnish (optional)

When roasted with a generous amount of extra-virgin olive oil, artichokes will develop a sweet, buttery flavor with undertones of their natural flavor. Be very delicate with the artichokes when you're peeling them so they don't break apart in your hands.

1. Preheat the oven to 375 degrees, positioning the rack in the center of the oven.

2. Cut the artichokes in half, peel away their outer layers, and remove the hairs in the center.

3. Spread the artichoke halves evenly across the surface of a rimmed backing sheet, cut side up.

4. In a small bowl, mix together the extra-virgin olive oil, garlic, and lemon juice. Whisk well and then pour over the artichokes. Season with a bit of the coarsely ground black pepper and fresh sea salt. Flip the halves so that they lay cut side down.

5. Transfer the baking sheet to the oven and cook for about 40 minutes, until the artichokes are lightly charred and tender. Remove from the oven and serve warm, garnishing with rosemary if desired.

SPICED CORN

MAKES 6 SERVINGS
ACTIVE TIME: 10 MINUTES
TOTAL TIME: 20 MINUTES

2 tablespoons
unsalted butter

6 ears corn, husks
removed and kernels
separated

½ teaspoon cayenne
pepper

¼ teaspoon an-
cho chile pepper

1 teaspoon
coarsely ground
black pepper

1 teaspoon fresh
sea salt

Inspired by several Southern-style dishes we prepared at the White Barn Inn in Kennebunk, Maine, when I worked there, Spiced Corn takes on that Southern flavor with the ancho chile powder and cayenne pepper. It's important to use a seasoned cast-iron skillet with this recipe so the corn will become both buttery and crisp.

1. Place a medium cast-iron skillet over medium-high heat.

2. Add the butter to the pan and when hot, add the corn, cayenne pepper, ancho chile pepper, coarsely ground black pepper, and fresh sea salt. Cook the corn for about 15 minutes, stirring frequently.

3. Remove the skillet from the heat and serve immediately.

FOIL-ROASTED RED BEETS

MAKES 6 SERVINGS
ACTIVE TIME: 20 MINUTES
TOTAL TIME: 55 MINUTES

2 tablespoons extra-virgin olive oil

2 sprigs fresh thyme, leaves removed

2 teaspoons coarsely ground black pepper

2 teaspoons fresh sea salt

8 to 10 medium beets, cleaned and scrubbed

When roasting beets with foil, the foil serves as a second heating system that encourages the beets to be cooked evenly. All you need for this recipe is a couple spoonfuls of extra-virgin olive oil and some thyme, two flavors that truly go hand-in-hand with the earthy flavors of the beets.

1. Preheat the oven to 400 degrees, positioning the rack in the center of the oven.

2. In a small bowl, combine the extra-virgin olive oil, thyme, coarsely ground black pepper, and fresh sea salt. Set aside.

3. Brush the beets with the thyme and olive oil marinade. Next, wrap each beet with a sheet of aluminum foil and then place on a baking sheet.

4. Transfer to oven and cook for about 45 minutes, until the beets can be easily pierced with a fork. Remove from the oven and let cool.

5. When cool enough, cut the tops and bottoms off the beets and peel away the skin. Slice into ¼-inch strips and serve warm.

MASALA RICE WITH PEAS & TOMATOES

MAKES 6 SERVINGS
ACTIVE TIME: 35 MINUTES
TOTAL TIME: 1 HOUR AND 30 MINUTES

2 tablespoons extra-virgin olive oil

1 medium white onion, finely chopped

2 teaspoons minced fresh ginger

3 garlic cloves, minced

2 plum tomatoes, chopped into ¼-inch cubes

½ cup fresh peas

2 teaspoons curry powder

2 cups chicken broth

1½ cups uncooked jasmine rice

1 tablespoon coarsely ground black pepper

1 tablespoon fresh sea salt

Inspired by Indian flavors, Masala Rice with Peas & Tomatoes goes best when paired with the Rotisserie-Grilled Prime Rib (page 98). Serve alongside some Roasted Tomatoes with Rosemary & Olive Oil (page 200).

1. Preheat the oven to 400 degrees, positioning the rack in the center of the oven.

2. Add the extra-virgin olive oil to a medium saucepan that's oven-safe and place over medium heat. When hot, add the white onion and ginger and cook about 7 minutes, until translucent. Stir in the garlic and cook for another 2 minutes, until golden.

3. Next, stir in the tomatoes, peas, curry powder, and chicken broth and bring to a boil. Remove from the heat when the broth begins to boil.

4. Add the rice, pepper, and salt to the saucepan and transfer to the oven. Cook for about 1 hour, until the rice is soft and cooked through. Remove from the oven and serve warm.

GLUTEN GF FREE

ROASTED TOMATOES WITH ROSEMARY & OLIVE OIL

MAKES 6 SERVINGS
ACTIVE TIME: 20 MINUTES
TOTAL TIME: 1 HOUR

8 large plum tomatoes, halved

3 tablespoons extra-virgin olive oil

3 sprigs fresh rosemary, leaves separated

1 sprig fresh thyme, leaves separated

Coarsely ground black pepper

Fresh sea salt

Extremely simple though flavorful, roasted tomatoes are always wonderful when the skin is slightly charred and the olive oil has seeped into the cavities of the tomato halves. Sometimes I'll even put these under the broiler for a minute or two at the end of the roasting process so the tomatoes develop a blistered skin.

1. Preheat the oven to 375 degrees, positioning the rack in the center of the oven.

2. Spread the halved tomatoes across a rimmed baking sheet. Next, drizzle the extra-virgin olive oil over the tomatoes, followed by the rosemary and thyme leaves. Season with the coarsely ground black pepper and fresh sea salt, and then transfer to the oven. Roast for 45 minutes to 1 hour, until the skins are wrinkled.

3. Remove the baking sheet from the oven and let the tomatoes cool while still on the baking sheet. Serve warm or at room temperature.

LEMON & PARSLEY RISOTTO

MAKES 6 SERVINGS
ACTIVE TIME: 35 MINUTES
TOTAL TIME: 1 HOUR

3 tablespoons unsalted butter

1 medium white onion, chopped

2 garlic cloves, minced

2 cups Arborio rice

½ cup dry white wine

5 cups chicken broth

¼ medium lemon, juiced

1 cup freshly grated Parmesan cheese

¼ cup flat-leaf parsley, finely chopped

Coarsely ground black pepper

Fresh sea salt

More of an Italian dish, Lemon & Parsley Risotto is perfect when paired with the Rotisserie-Grilled Prime Rib (page 98) on a summer evening. To attain the perfect consistency in risotto, you must take it very slow, adding the chicken broth to the risotto half a cup at a time. And because white wine is a central component to this risotto, you can serve with white wine as well.

1. Place a tall cast-iron skillet or saucepan over medium heat. Add the butter to the pan and when hot, add the onion and garlic and cook about 3 minutes, until the onion is translucent and the garlic is golden.

2. Add the rice to the skillet and cook for 2 to 3 minutes. Next, add the wine and cook until ¾ of it is reduced and absorbed into the rice. Note that the rice will begin to look thickened.

3. Slowly mix in the chicken broth ½ cup at a time, so that it is absorbed before adding more. This will take about 35 minutes. When the liquid is fully absorbed and the rice creamy, remove the pan from the heat.

4. While the rice is still hot, stir in the lemon juice, Parmesan cheese, and parsley, and then season with the coarsely ground black pepper and fresh sea salt. Serve warm.

BREADS

SERVED ALONGSIDE AN OPEN CUT OF PRIME RIB, WARMED ROLLS OR A FRESH LOAF OF SOURDOUGH TO BE SLICED AND SHARED WITH THE FAMILY IS A PERFECT ADDITION TO A GENTLE HOLIDAY EVENING. The snaps and crackles that sound when a serrated knife cuts through a loaf reminds me of Christmas evening, with my mother's prime rib at the center of the table. On top of everything she does throughout the entire day of Christmas, she somehow always manages to make her own loaf of sourdough with a starter she has been cultivating for the week or two preceding the evening.

There's nothing quite like a sourdough made with your own starter. A starter is essentially the process of growing the yeast that's necessary to make the bread rise. No two starters are exactly alike, primarily because the nature of the yeast's development is largely influenced by the atmosphere it's grown in—the temperature, humidity, sunlight, water acidity, etc. Although this sounds fairly complicated, it really isn't.

Mixing together equal parts room-temperature water with a 1:1 ratio of whole-wheat and all-purpose flour over the course of one to two weeks creates your starter. It should always be fed each morning and then kept in a shady spot for the remainder of the day and night. Feeding the starter involves discarding about three quarters of yesterday's starter, and then adding a fresh ratio of flour and water back into the bowl or cup (you want this to be glass, plastic, or stainless steel so that its surface doesn't interfere with the yeast's development).

The importance of a fresh starter cannot be overstated. You may be able to purchase a starter from your local baker the day before you plan to bake, or you may be able to find a dry starter (King Arthur makes a good one) at your local supermarket, which may be the simplest method because all you'll need from there is a little bit of water. But there's nothing like the process of feeding a starter—it doesn't need to be exact, and the starter will always forgive you if you add too much or too little water or flour once or twice. I really encourage you to give it a shot by following the recipe on page 206.

SOURDOUGH STARTER

50/50 mixture all-purpose and whole-wheat flour

Water at room temperature

1. In a small glass, plastic, or stainless steel bowl, combine equal amounts of water and flour—I would say about 1 cup of each. Use a spoon and whisk it together thoroughly, scraping off the dough that lines the sides. Cover with a towel and place in a shady area at room temperature. Let rest for 2 to 3 days.

2. When you uncover the starter in the morning 2 to 3 days later, it may have risen slightly and bubbles will appear on the surface. If a dried layer of flour appears on the surface, peel it back and discard.

3. Discard about three quarters of the starter and then replace it with equal amounts water and flour so that you recreate the original amount. Cover and return to a shady environment, and let rest overnight.

4. Repeat the process for about 1 to 2 weeks, until the starter has a bubbly surface and starts to smell slightly sour; when you obverse it over the course of a day, it should rise just after being fed, and then fall throughout the afternoon and night.

5. Your starter is now ready. For most of the recipes that follow, you will need only 1 cup of the starter. When you take the cup of starter from the original batch, be sure to feed the starter again to its normal amount. When it starts to get bubbly, transfer the starter to the refrigerator so the growing process is halted and you can return to it several days later, before planning to bake again.

COUNTRY SOURDOUGH

MAKES 8 SERVINGS
ACTIVE TIME: 2 HOURS
TOTAL TIME: 6 TO 12 HOURS

⅔ cup active starter

1 cup water, room temperature

2 tablespoons extra-virgin olive oil

2¼ cup 50/50 whole-wheat and all-purpose flour (see opposite page)

2 teaspoons fresh sea salt

For Country Sourdough, your starter will largely determine the actual acidity and density of the bread, though the best part of any sourdough is the crust. Baking with the Dutch oven allows for a two-step process: at first the Dutch oven is covered, allowing for a consistent temperature, and then it's uncovered so that the loaf undergoes its final rise and the crust takes its shape. Be sure to let the finished loaf rest on a cooling rack for 15 minutes before carving with a serrated knife, as this will give the crust several additional minutes of cooking.

1. In a large plastic, glass, or stainless steel bowl, combine the starter, water, extra-virgin olive oil, and flour using your hands. Make sure all the flour is incorporated into the dough, and then set aside and let rest for 30 minutes.

2. Next, fold the salt thoroughly into the dough and continue to fold until the dough takes the shape of a ball. Cover the bowl with plastic wrap and place in an area that receives an average amount of sunlight. This is the bulk fermentation process, and you should let the dough rest anywhere from 4 hours to overnight, until it has practically doubled in size. If you'd like to increase the volume (and essentially the density of the bread after it's baked), fold the bread over itself every 20 minutes for the first couple hours of the bulk fermentation. Simply lift one edge of the dough and fold it on top of the other.

3. Dust a large carving board with a handful of flour and then transfer the dough from the bowl to the carving board. Using a bread spatula, fold all four edges of the dough to the center and then flip the entire loaf upside down, so that the seams of the folded dough press onto the carving board. Continue to do this until the dough begins to rise and take a round shape.

4. Place the shaped dough inside a large bowl lined with a floured kitchen towel, seam side down. Let rest for 1 to 3 hours, until it rises significantly.

5. Coat the inside of a medium Dutch oven with flour, and then preheat the oven to 400 degrees.

6. After the dough has risen, transfer the loaf from the bowl to the Dutch oven, and then cover and transfer to the oven. Bake for 20 minutes. Remove the lid and then bake for about 35 more minutes, until the loaf is golden brown and crisp.

7. Remove the loaf from the Dutch oven immediately and let rest for about 15 minutes before slicing.

PULL-APART BREAD

I have altered this recipe so that it gives you two options: you can bake your own Country Sourdough (page 207), or you can go to a local baker and pick up an artisanal loaf. A cheesy pull-apart bread is perfect when you take a piece and dip it in some fresh au jus that comes from a cut of rib roast.

MAKES 8 SERVINGS
ACTIVE TIME: 30 MINUTES
TOTAL TIME: 50 MINUTES

1 loaf Country Sourdough (page 207), or any artisanal sourdough

2 cups shredded cheese of your choice

¼ cup coarsely chopped bacon

Coarsely ground black pepper (optional)

Fresh sea salt

¼ cup melted unsalted butter

1. Preheat the oven to 350 degrees.

2. Cut the bread into 1-inch cubes. To do so, place it on a large carving board alongside a serrated knife. Level the knife evenly across the top of the loaf, and then cut down vertically, leaving about 1½ inches from the bottom up uncut. Do this across the loaf, so that you form 1-inch columns.

3. Then, rotate the bread 90 degrees. Again, cut the loaf vertically into 1-inch strips, leaving the bottom untouched. This will allow the bread to have a solid foundation.

4. In a small bowl, combine the shredded cheese, bacon, coarsely ground black pepper and fresh sea salt and mix thoroughly. Using your hands, stuff the cheesy mixture in between the cracks of the loaf.

5. Place the loaf on a baking sheet and then drizzle the melted butter on top of the loaf. Optional: Coarsely crack some black pepper over the loaf, along with some coarse sea salt.

6. Transfer the loaf to the oven and bake about 20 minutes, until the cheese has melted.

7. Remove from the oven and serve immediately.

WHEAT LOAF WITH CARAMELIZED ONIONS & BLACK OLIVES

MAKES 8 SERVINGS
ACTIVE TIME: 2 HOURS
TOTAL TIME: 12 TO 14 HOURS

½ large white onion

3 tablespoons extra-virgin olive oil

1 cup black olives, pitted and halved

¼ teaspoon instant yeast

1½ cups water

2 cups whole-wheat flour

1 cup all-purpose flour

Fresh sea salt

A classic wheat loaf is slightly more complex than Country Sourdough (page 207) and requires additional time during the bulk fermentation period. In Country Sourdough, the fermentation period is much more variant (largely dependent upon your starter) spanning from 4 hours to overnight, while a wheat loaf requires at least 12 hours because of its unprocessed grains. Here I've substitute the starter with ¼ teaspoon of instant yeast, and I've added additional flavors like caramelized onions and black olives to give you an idea of how you can alter these foundational recipes.

1. On a large carving board, peel and chop off the ends of your onion. Next, slice it into ¼-inch strips and set aside.

2. Place a medium cast-iron skillet over low heat and add 1 tablespoon of the extra-virgin olive oil to the pan. When hot, add the strips of onion and begin the caramelizing process. Simply sauté the onion strips for about 30 minutes, stirring every minute or so. Let the onions naturally stick to the pan so that they become brown and extra tender. When finished, remove from pan and let cool.

3. Mix the cooled caramelized onions with the black olives. Set aside.

4. In a large bowl, mix the water and the yeast and let rest until the yeast has dissolved fully, about 5 minutes. Using your hands, stir in the flour and a pinch of sea salt. When mixed thoroughly, cover the bowl with a kitchen towel, transfer to the corner of the kitchen, and then let rest overnight until the dough has risen significantly. If you would like to increase the volume (and essentially the density of the bread after it's baked), fold the dough over itself every 20 minutes for the first couple hours of the bulk fermentation. Simply lift one edge of the dough and fold it on top of the other.

5. Dust a large carving board with a handful of flour and then transfer the dough from the bowl to the carving board. Carefully add the caramelized onions and olives to the dough and then, using a bread spatula, fold all four edges of the dough to the center and then flip the entire loaf upside down, so that the seams of the folded dough press onto the carving board. Continue to do this until the dough begins to rise and take on a round shape.

6. Place the shaped dough inside a large bowl lined with a floured kitchen towel, seam side down. Let rest for 1 to 3 hours, until it rises significantly.

7. Place a large sheet pan in the oven and preheat the oven to 400 degrees.

8. After the dough has risen, remove the hot sheet pan from the oven and carefully coat it with the remaining extra virgin olive oil. Next, transfer the dough to the sheet pan and then to the oven. Bake for 30 to 45 minutes, until the loaf is golden brown.

9. Remove the loaf from the oven and let rest for about 15 minutes before slicing.

CHEESE, HERB & GARLIC BREAD

MAKES 8 SERVINGS
ACTIVE TIME: 20 MINUTES
TOTAL TIME: 35 MINUTES

1 loaf Country Sour-
dough (page 207), or
any artisanal sour-
dough

6 garlic cloves, minced

1 tablespoon flat-leaf
parsley, finely chopped

1 tablespoon fresh rose-
mary, finely chopped

½ cup (1 stick) unsalted
butter, softened

1 cup 50/50 blend moz-
zarella and Parmesan
cheeses

Coarsely ground black
pepper

Fresh sea salt

As with the pull-apart bread, here you have the option to bake your own sour-dough or pick up a loaf from your local baker, though I encourage you to try your own if only for the experience. With the cooking times provided here in this recipe, the slices of sourdough will be extra crisp and browned, and the cheese, mixed with the garlic and herbs, will be melted into the bread's crevices.

1. Preheat your oven to 375 degrees.

2. Cut the bread into ¼- to ½-inch slices.

3. In a small bowl, combine the garlic, parsley, and rosemary with the softened butter and mix thoroughly.

4. Using the back of a spoon, thoroughly press and apply the garlic and herb butter to the slices of sourdough. Transfer the slices of bread to a baking sheet lined with aluminum foil, and then to the oven. Bake for about 15 minutes, until crisp, and then remove from the oven.

5. Bring the oven to 450 degrees.

6. Distribute the cheese onto the slices of garlic bread, and then season with a little coarsely ground black pepper and fresh sea salt. Transfer back into the oven and cook for another 10 minutes or so, until the cheese has melted thoroughly over the bread.

7. Remove from the oven and serve immediately.

WHOLE GRAIN LOAF WITH ROSEMARY & LEMON

MAKES 8 SERVINGS
ACTIVE TIME: 2 HOURS
TOTAL TIME: 12 TO 14 HOURS

1½ cups lukewarm water

¼ teaspoon instant yeast

2 cups whole-grain flour

1 cup all-purpose flour

2 teaspoons fresh rosemary, finely chopped

2 teaspoons lemon zest

¼ cup rolled oats

Pinch fresh sea salt

Perhaps the most compatible flavor with prime rib is rosemary, and what goes best with rosemary? Lemon. Here I've taken a traditional whole grain loaf and added in some finely chopped rosemary and lemon zest. As with the Wheat Loaf (page 210), this takes a longer amount of time compared to the Country Sourdough (page 207), because the unprocessed grains require a much longer time during the bulk fermentation process. Before serving, cut the bread into long, crisp slices and slather with some Herbed Butter (page 154).

1. In a large bowl, mix the water and yeast and let rest for about 5 minutes, until the yeast has fully dissolved, Using your hands, knead in the flour, rosemary, lemon zest, oats, and sea salt. Cover the bowl with a kitchen towel, transfer to a shady corner of the kitchen, and let rest overnight, until the dough has risen significantly.

2. Dust a large carving board with a handful of flour and then transfer the dough from the bowl to the carving board. Using a bread spatula, fold all four edges of the dough to the center and then flip the entire loaf upside down, so that the seams of the folded dough press onto the carving board.

3. Place the shaped dough inside a large bowl lined with a floured kitchen towel, seam side down. Let rest for 2 hours, until it doubles in size.

4. Place a large Dutch oven in the oven and preheat the oven to 450 degrees.

5. Remove the Dutch oven from the oven and coat with flour. Next, carefully scoop the dough out of the bowl and place it in the Dutch oven, seam side up. Cover the Dutch oven and transfer to the oven, and cook for 25 to 30 minutes. Remove the top and cook for about 15 to 20 more minutes, until the loaf is golden brown.

6. Remove the loaf from the oven and let rest for about 15 minutes before slicing.

COUNTRY ROLLS

MAKES AT LEAST 8 SERV-INGS
ACTIVE TIME: 1 HOUR
TOTAL TIME: 2 HOURS AND 15 MINUTES

⅓ cup warm water

1 packet active dry yeast

4 cups all-purpose flour

1 cup warm whole milk

3 tablespoons unsalted butter, melted

2 tablespoons sugar

Fresh sea salt

Because of the sugar and milk that are prominent ingredients to most rolls, the bulk fermentation process is only about 1 to 2 hours. Shaping the rolls takes a little getting used to, though once you get the hang of it, it'll come naturally. Depending upon how you prefer your rolls to be—individual or pull-apart—the dish you cook them in is key. I prefer to use a classic sheet pan, separating the rolls so that each becomes the diner's own. However, if you'd like to make pull-apart rolls, take a deep baking pan, slather with butter, and place your shaped dough balls firmly side by side one another, allowing the rolls to bake both individually and also as one loaf.

1. In a large bowl, mix the water and yeast and let rest for about 5 minutes, until the yeast has fully dissolved.

2. Next, using an electric mixer equipped with a dough paddle, mix the water and yeast, flour, whole milk, unsalted butter, sugar, and a pinch of sea salt. Mix thoroughly for about 5 minutes, until the dough is thick and clings to the dough hook.

3. Remove the dough from the mixing bowl and transfer to a floured bowl. Cover with a kitchen towel and let rest in a shady corner of the kitchen for 1 to 2 hours, until the dough has doubled in size.

4. Preheat the oven to 375 degrees.

5. Dust a large carving board with a handful of flour and then transfer the dough from the bowl to the carving board. Slowly pick off small pieces of the dough and, using your hands, form into three-inch balls. Place the balls of dough onto a large, greased baking sheet. You may need more than one.

6. Transfer the baking sheet(s) to the oven and bake until the rolls are golden and they give off a hollow sound when tapped.

7. Remove from the oven and let cool 10 minutes before serving.

YORKSHIRE PUDDING

MAKES 6 SERVINGS
ACTIVE TIME: 15 MINUTES
TOTAL TIME: 35 MINUTES

6 tablespoons canola oil

1 cup flour

3 medium eggs

1 cup whole milk

½ teaspoon fresh sea salt

While Yorkshire Pudding boasts the same elemental ingredients (flour and eggs minus the yeast) as many breads, what makes it different is the batter is baked like a muffin. Crisp though doughy, these go great when served alongside a slice of prime rib with au jus poured into the little crevices that form atop each pudding.

1. Preheat the oven to 450 degrees.

2. Place one tablespoon of the canola oil into each hole of a 6-hole muffin tray, making sure it coats all the sides, and then transfer the tray to the oven.

3. Add the flour to the medium bowl and using a wooden spatula, slowly fold the eggs into the flour. Next, gradually whisk in the milk making sure all lumps are removed. Let rest for 15 minutes.

4. Remove the muffin tray with the hot oil and add an equal amount of batter into each of the holes. Transfer back to the oven and cook for 23 to 25 minutes, until the batter has become golden and puffy. Remove and serve immediately.

IRISH SODA BREAD

MAKES 6 TO 8 SERVINGS
ACTIVE TIME: 30 MINUTES
TOTAL TIME: 1 HOUR

3½ cups flour

½ cup granulated sugar

1 teaspoon baking soda

2 teaspoons baking powder

1 teaspoon fresh sea salt

4 tablespoons (½ stick) unsalted butter

1¼ cups buttermilk, chilled

2 eggs

¾ cup raisins

GLAZED CRUST

3 tablespoons hot milk

¾ cup powdered sugar

1 teaspoon vanilla extract

Irish Soda Bread was originally the standard tabletop loaf of bread in Ireland. It became so popular because of its simple ingredients: buttermilk, flour, eggs, and baking soda. Later, when Irish immigrants came to America, Irish Soda Bread took on more of an upscale ingredient list to incorporate raisins and seeds. In Ireland, Soda Bread is never kneaded but is rather mixed together in a medium bowl. I always serve this after the main dish as a sort of dessert bread.

1. Preheat the oven to 375 degrees.

2. With an electric mixer, combine the flour, sugar, baking soda, baking powder, and salt. Slowly add the butter in 1-tablespoon pieces. Transfer the dough from the mixing bowl to a separate bowl.

3. With a wooden spatula, fold in the buttermilk and eggs, followed by the raisins.

4. Remove the dough from the bowl with your hands and form into a tight, round loaf. Place the loaf on a baking sheet lined with parchment paper, and then using the blunt edge of a knife, carve an X into the top of the loaf—this will allow for thorough baking.

5. Transfer the baking sheet to the oven and bake for 45 minutes, until you can pierce a knife through the bread's center and it comes out clean.

6. Remove from the oven and let rest for 10 minutes before slicing, allowing the crust to harden with the cool temperature.

VARIATION: FOR AN IRISH SODA BREAD WITH A GLAZED CRUST, FOLLOW THESE INSTRUCTIONS:

Whisk together the hot milk with powdered sugar and vanilla extract.

A minute before removing the bread from the oven, brush the glaze on top of the loaf. Remove from the oven and let rest for 10 minutes before slicing.

DESSERTS

DESSERT MAY BE THE LAST THING ON YOUR MIND AFTER A RICH AND HEARTY PRIME RIB DINNER, BUT TAKE A PAUSE BETWEEN COURSES FOR A SIP OF WINE AND SOME LIGHT CONVERSATION JUST TO SAVE SOME ROOM FOR ANY OF THESE SWEET TREATS.

From traditional favorites like Cheesecake and Molasses Cookies to lighter fare like Poached Pears and Baked Stuffed Apples and decadent delights like Chocolate Caramel Pecan Pie and Chocolate Nut Torte, we've got a dozen dessert options sure to finish a prime rib dinner in style. You'll find it hard to say "no" to these meal enders. Just as in the rest of this book, the focus is on farm-fresh ingredients, with several fruit-based desserts as well as those that give the spotlight over to nuts, dairy products, chocolate, real maple syrup, or natural peanut butter. Several of the recipes can be made in your slow cooker—especially convenient if your oven has been occupied by prime rib. And if you're going gluten-free, half of our desserts are flour-less. Because no one should have to forgo dessert.

POACHED PEARS

MAKES 4 TO 6 SERVINGS
ACTIVE TIME: 15 MINUTES
TOTAL TIME: 2 TO 5 HOURS

4 to 6 ripe pears, peeled, halved, and cored

1 cup red wine

¾ cup granulated sugar

1 3-inch cinnamon stick

2 3-inch strips orange zest

A simple pear, poached in red wine scented with cinnamon and orange zest, is a perfect ending for a winter meal. Serve with some biscotti to add crunch. Note: This dish can be prepared up to 2 days in advance and refrigerated, tightly covered.

1. Arrange the pears in a slow cooker; cut them into quarters, if necessary, to make them fit.

2. In a mixing bowl, combine the red wine and sugar. Stir well to dissolve the sugar, and pour the mixture over the pears. Add the cinnamon stick and orange zest to the slow cooker.

3. Cook on Low for 4 to 5 hours or on High for 2 to 2½ hours, until pears are tender when pierced with a fork. Remove and discard the cinnamon stick and orange zest. Allow pears to cool in the poaching liquid, and serve warm or chilled.

VARIATIONS:

• Substitute sweet Marsala for the red wine, and reduce the amount of sugar to ½ cup.

• Substitute white wine for the red wine, lemon zest for the orange zest, and omit the cinnamon stick.

• Substitute ripe peaches for the pears.

TIP: CORE HALVED PEARS WITH A MELON BALLER, LEAVING A NEAT, ROUND HOLE.

BERRY-PEACH COBBLER

MAKES 4 SERVINGS
ACTIVE TIME: 20 MINUTES
TOTAL TIME: 2 TO 5 HOURS

1 cup all-purpose flour

¾ cup brown sugar

1 teaspoon baking powder

¼ teaspoon salt

¼ teaspoon ground cinnamon

¼ teaspoon ground nutmeg

2 eggs, lightly beaten

3 tablespoons vegetable oil

2 tablespoons low-fat milk

4 cups fresh or frozen berries

2 cups fresh or frozen peaches, diced

1 cup water

3 tablespoons quick-cooking tapioca

½ cup maple syrup

This time-tested favorite makes for a great meal-ender, especially in the summertime when you can swap out frozen berries for fresh ones!

1. In a medium bowl, stir together the flour, brown sugar, baking powder, salt, cinnamon, and nutmeg. In a small bowl, combine the eggs, vegetable oil, and milk. Add the egg mixture all at once to the flour mixture. Stir until just moistened. Set aside.

2. In a large saucepan, combine the berries and peaches, water, and tapioca. Bring to a boil. Add maple syrup to the hot fruit mixture, remove from the heat, and add to a slow cooker. Immediately spoon the batter over the fruit mixture.

3. Cover and cook on Low for 4 to 5 hours or on High for 1 to 2 hours. Test for doneness by inserting a toothpick in the center. If it comes out clean, it's done. When done, turn the slow cooker off, leave uncovered, and let stand for 30 minutes to 1 hour to cool. Serve warm.

BAKED STUFFED APPLES

MAKES 4 TO 6 SERVINGS
ACTIVE TIME: 15 MINUTES
TOTAL TIME: 2 TO 5 HOURS

½ cup chopped walnuts

4 to 6 baking apples, such as Jonathan or Northern Spy

½ cup crushed almond biscotti

2 tablespoons unsalted butter, melted

½ cup dry white wine

¼ cup granulated sugar

Baked apples are appreciated in every country, and this Italian version includes some crunchy nuts and flavorful biscotti as part of the stuffing. Note: This dish can be prepared up to 2 days in advance and refrigerated, tightly covered.

1. Preheat the oven to 350 degrees, and line a baking sheet with aluminum foil.

2. Place the walnuts on the baking sheet and toast for 5 to 7 minutes, until browned. Set aside.

3. Core the apples and peel the top half only. Arrange the apples in a slow cooker.

4. In a small bowl, combine the nuts, biscotti, and melted butter. Spoon equal portions of the mixture into the empty cores of the apples.

5. In a mixing bowl, combine the white wine and sugar, and stir well to dissolve sugar. Spoon the wine mixture over the apples.

6. Cook on Low for 4 to 6 hours or on High for 2 to 3 hours, until apples are tender when pierced with a fork. Serve hot, at room temperature, or chilled.

VARIATION: SUBSTITUTE ORANGE MARMALADE FOR THE SUGAR, AND ADD TWO 3-INCH STRIPS OF ORANGE ZEST TO THE SLOW COOKER.

TIP: BE SURE TO PEEL THE TOP HALF OF THE APPLE. IF YOU DON'T, STEAM BUILDS UP INSIDE THE SKIN AND THE APPLE TENDS TO FALL APART.

MOLASSES COOKIES

By Alexandra Lewis

If you're preparing a holiday season feast, these chewy molasses cookies should be your go-to dessert. The extra kick of ginger makes them feel especially festive!

1. Preheat the oven to 375 degrees and line a baking sheet with parchment paper.

2. In a large bowl, cream together the butter, sugar, egg, and molasses.

3. In a medium bowl, mix flour, baking soda, cinnamon, ginger, cloves, and salt.

4. Add the dry ingredients to the molasses mixture and stir to combine.

5. Chill the dough for 1 hour.

6. Shape the chilled dough into rounded tablespoonfuls, roll in the white sugar, and place on the parchment-lined baking sheet, at least 1 inch apart.

7. Bake the cookies for 10 minutes, until just set.

8. Remove from the oven and let cool on a wire cooling rack.

MAKES ABOUT 12 COOKIES, DEPENDING ON THE SIZE
ACTIVE TIME: 15 MINUTES
TOTAL TIME: 25 MINUTES

¾ cup (1½ sticks) unsalted butter

1 cup packed brown sugar

1 egg

⅓ cup molasses

2 cups flour

2 teaspoons baking soda

1 teaspoon cinnamon

1 teaspoon ginger

½ teaspoon cloves

¼ teaspoon salt

¼ cup white sugar, set aside in a bowl for rolling

FLOURLESS PEANUT BUTTER COOKIES

By Alexandra Lewis

Like a classic prime rib, these cookies are insanely good. You won't believe they're flourless.

MAKES ABOUT 12 COOKIES, DEPENDING ON THE SIZE
ACTIVE TIME: 15 MINUTES
TOTAL TIME: 25 MINUTES

1 cup natural peanut butter

1 egg

⅔ cup white sugar

⅓ cup brown sugar

1 teaspoon baking powder

¼ cup white sugar, set aside in a bowl for rolling

1. Preheat oven to 350 degrees and line a baking sheet with parchment paper.

2. In a large bowl, combine all the ingredients except the ¼ cup white sugar for rolling.

3. Shape the dough into rounded tablespoonfuls, roll in the white sugar, and place on the parchment-lined baking sheet, at least 1 inch apart.

4. Crosshatch the top of each cookie by pressing a fork down into the dough horizontally and then vertically.

5. Bake the cookies for 10 minutes, until they start to slightly brown on the edges.

6. Remove from the oven and let cool on a wire cooling rack.

VARIATION: ADD ¼ CUP MINI CHOCOLATE CHIPS TO THE DOUGH.

ALMOND-COCONUT CAKE

By Alexandra Lewis

MAKES 8 SMALL SERVINGS
ACTIVE TIME: 20 MINUTES
TOTAL TIME: 50 MINUTES

¾ cup (1½ sticks) salted butter

¾ cup sugar

4 eggs

1 teaspoon vanilla

½ cup cream (or full-fat coconut milk, for a richer coconut flavor)

1½ cup almond meal

¼ cup coconut flour

¼ cup all-purpose flour

2 teaspoon baking soda

¼ cup shredded, sweetened coconut

Powdered sugar, for dusting

Blueberries or whipped cream, to serve (optional)

If you're looking for something soft, moist, and succulent that won't sit too heavy after a prime rib meal, give this delicious Almond-Coconut Cake a try. Top with powdered sugar and some fresh blueberries if they're in season, and even try a dollop of whipped cream on top, if you're feeling decadent!

1. Preheat the oven to 350 degrees and grease a round cake pan.

2. In a medium bowl, cream the butter and sugar with an electric beater until smooth.

3. In a small bowl, beat the eggs. Add beaten eggs to the butter-sugar mixture and thoroughly combine. Add the vanilla and cream, and combine thoroughly.

4. In a large bowl, combine the almond meal, flours, and baking soda, and mix well.

5. Add the wet ingredients to the dry ingredients and beat with the electric mixer.

6. Add the coconut, and mix well.

7. Spread the batter evenly into the greased pan, and bake for 30 minutes, until the edges begin to turn gold and a knife inserted comes out clean.

8. Remove from the oven and let cool on a wire cooling rack. Slice into wedges. Dust with powdered sugar to serve, and top with blueberries or a dollop of whipped cream.

THIS CAN EASILY BE MADE GLUTEN-FREE BY REPLACING THE ALL-PURPOSE FLOUR WITH WHITE RICE FLOUR FOR EQUALLY DELICIOUS RESULTS.

UPSIDE-DOWN CARAMEL PEAR TART

YIELD: 6 TO 8 SERVINGS
ACTIVE TIME: 20 MINUTES
TOTAL TIME: 50 MINUTES

6 tablespoons (¾ stick) unsalted butter

1½ cups granulated sugar

6 pears, peeled, cored, and quartered, with each quarter halved lengthwise

3 tablespoons freshly squeezed lemon juice

¼ teaspoon cinnamon

¼ teaspoon nutmeg

1 frozen pie crust

This upside-down pie, called a tarte tatin in classic French cooking, is the ultimate showy dessert but quite easy to make. It's also speedier than a pie because the fruit is basically cooked on top of the stove before a final baking.

1. Melt the butter in 12-inch cast-iron or other ovenproof skillet over medium-high heat. Stir in 1 cup of the sugar and cook, stirring frequently, for 6 to 8 minutes, until the caramel is a deep walnut brown. Remove the pan from the heat, and set aside.

2. Place pear slices in mixing bowl, and toss with the remaining sugar, lemon juice, cinnamon, and nutmeg. Let rest for 15 minutes.

3. Preheat the oven to 425 degrees.

4. Drain the pear slices, and arrange them tightly in a decorative pattern on top of the caramel. Place any remaining pear slices on top of the decorative base. Place pan over medium-high heat, and press down on the pears as they begin to soften.

5. Using a bulb baster, draw up juices from the pears and pour juices over the pears as they cook. Do not stir them. After 5 minutes, or when pears begin to soften, cover the pan, and cook the pears for 10 to 15 minutes more, until the pears are soft and the liquid is thick. During this time, continue to baste the pears.

6. Take the pan off the heat, and form the pie crust dough into a circle 1 inch or larger than the circumference of the pan. Lay over the pan and tuck the ends around the pears on the sides of the pan using the tip of a paring knife. Cut six 1-inch slits in top of the dough to allow steam to release.

7. Bake the tart in the oven for 20 minutes, until the pastry is golden and the juices are thick.

8. Remove the pan from the oven, and let cool for 10 minutes. Using a knife, loosen the edges of the tart from the pan. Invert a serving plate over the pan and then, holding the pan and the plate together firmly, invert them. Lift off the pan. Replace any pears that might have stuck to the bottom of the pan neatly on top of the tart. Serve warm or at room temperature.

CHOCOLATE NUT TORTE

YIELD: 8 SERVINGS
ACTIVE TIME: 15 MINUTES
TOTAL TIME: 1½ HOURS,
INCLUDING 1 HOUR FOR
CHILLING

10 ounces bittersweet chocolate, chopped and divided

2 cups pecan or walnut halves, toasted in a 350 degree oven for 5 minutes

2 tablespoons plus ½ cup granulated sugar

1 cup (2 sticks) unsalted butter, softened and divided

3 large eggs, at room temperature

1 tablespoon rum

The batter for this luscious chocolate cake is created in a matter of minutes in a food processor. It's a dense and rich cake that's crunchy with nuts and topped with a candy-like ganache. The torte can be prepared 1 day in advance and refrigerated. Allow it to reach room temperature before serving.

1. Preheat the oven to 375 degrees and grease an 8-inch round cake pan. Cut out a circle of wax or parchment paper, fit it into the bottom of the pan, and then grease the paper.

2. Melt 4 ounces of the chocolate in a microwave oven or over simmering water in a double boiler. Cool slightly.

3. Reserve 12 nut halves and chop the remaining nuts with 2 tablespoons of the sugar in a food processor fitted with a steel blade, using on-and-off pulsing. Scrape the nuts into a bowl.

4. Beat ½ cup (1 stick) of the butter and the remaining sugar in the food processor until light and fluffy. Add melted chocolate, then eggs, 1 at a time. Beat well between each addition, and scrape the sides of the work bowl with a rubber spatula. Add rum, then fold the chocolate mixture into the ground nuts.

5. Scrape batter into the prepared pan and bake for 25 minutes. The cake will be soft but firm up as it cools. Remove the cake from the oven and cool for 20 minutes on a wire cooling rack. Invert the cake onto a plate, remove the paper, and cool completely.

6. To make the glaze, combine the remaining 6 ounces of chocolate and remaining ½ cup (1 stick) of butter in a small saucepan. Melt over low heat and beat until shiny and smooth.

7. Place the cake on a wire rack over a sheet of wax paper. Pour the glaze over the center of the cake, and rotate the rack at an angle so the glaze runs down sides of the cake. Top with the 12 reserved nut halves, and allow to rest in a cool place until the chocolate hardens.

Variations

• Add 1 tablespoon of instant espresso powder to the batter.

• Substitute triple sec or Grand Marnier for the rum, and add 2 teaspoons of grated orange zest to the batter.

• Substitute blanched almonds for the pecans or walnuts, substitute amaretto for the rum, and add ½ teaspoon of pure almond extract to the batter.

TIP: IF YOU FIND THAT THE PARCHMENT PAPER STICKS TO THE TOP OF THE CAKE, BRUSH THE PAPER WITH A LITTLE WARM WATER. AFTER TEN SECONDS THE PAPER SHOULD PEEL RIGHT OFF.

CHEESECAKE

YIELD: 12 TO 16 SERVINGS
ACTIVE TIME: 20 MINUTES
TOTAL TIME: 6 HOURS, IN-
CLUDING CHILLING TIME

1½ cups graham cracker crumbs

5 tablespoons unsalted butter, melted

2 cups granulated sugar, divided

4 8-ounce packages cream cheese, softened

¼ cup flour

4 large eggs, at room temperature

2 large egg yolks, at room temperature

1 teaspoon pure vanilla extract

Pinch salt

Cheesecake is a perennial favorite—at the holidays or any time of the year. You can top it with fruit or a fruit sauce, or just enjoy it plain. Note: Cheesecake lasts forever! You can refrigerate this cake for up to 1 week; keep it tightly covered with plastic wrap.

1. Preheat the oven to 500 degrees.

2. In a mixing bowl, combine the graham cracker crumbs, butter, and ⅓ cup of the sugar, and stir well. Pat the mixture onto the bottom, and 1 inch up the sides, of a 12-inch springform pan. Set aside.

3. In a large mixing bowl, combine the remaining sugar, cream cheese, and flour, and beat at medium speed with an electric mixer until smooth. Add the eggs and egg yolks, one at a time, beating well between each addition, and scraping the sides of the bowl as necessary. Beat in the vanilla and salt. Scrape the mixture into the pan on top of the crust.

4. Bake in the center of the oven for 15 minutes. Reduce the oven temperature to 225 degrees and continue to bake the cheesecake for an additional 1 hour.

5. Turn off the oven, and allow the cheesecake to sit in the oven for an additional 30 minutes without opening the oven door.

6. Cool the cake in the pan on a wire cooling rack, and then refrigerate until cold. Run a knife around the sides of the pan to release cake, and then remove the sides of pan. Allow the cheesecake to sit at room temperature for 30 minutes before serving.

VARIATIONS

• Add 1 tablespoon of grated lemon or orange zest to the batter.

• Substitute firmly packed dark brown sugar for the granulated sugar in the batter.

• Mix ¼ of the batter with 3 tablespoons of unsweetened cocoa powder, and swirl this through the vanilla for a marble cheesecake.

CHOCOLATE ALMOND CHEESECAKE

YIELD: 8 TO 12 SERVINGS
ACTIVE TIME: 25 MINUTES
TOTAL TIME: 6 HOURS,
INCLUDING CHILLING TIME

1 cup slivered, blanched almonds

1½ cups graham cracker crumbs

¾ cup (1½ sticks) unsalted butter, melted and divided

9 ounces good-quality bittersweet chocolate, finely chopped and divided

2 8-ounce packages cream cheese, softened

½ cup sour cream

3 tablespoons amaretto or other almond-flavored liqueur

3 tablespoons flour

½ teaspoon pure almond extract

¼ teaspoon salt

2 large eggs, at room temperature

2/3 cup granulated sugar

Chocolate, cream cheese, and almonds are an unbeatable combination, especially in this dense and rich cheesecake. This cake can be made up to 4 days in advance and refrigerated, covered with plastic wrap. Allow it to sit at room temperature for 30 minutes before serving.

1. Preheat the oven to 350 degrees. Grease the bottom and sides of a 9-inch springform pan.

2. Place the almonds on a baking sheet, and toast for 5 to 7 minutes, until lightly browned.

3. Remove the pan from the oven, and finely chop the nuts in a food processor fitted with a steel blade, using on-and-off pulsing, or by hand.

4. In a mixing bowl, combine the graham cracker crumbs, 4 tablespoons of the butter, and 1 ounce of the chocolate, and stir well. Pat the mixture onto the bottom, and ½ inch up the sides, of the prepared pan. Bake the crust for 8 to 10 minutes, until lightly browned. Remove the crust and reduce the oven temperature to 325 degrees.

5. Melt the remaining chocolate in the remaining butter over low heat in a small pot or in the microwave in a microwave-safe bowl. Add the cream cheese, sour cream, amaretto, flour, almond extract, and salt. Beat for 1 minute on medium speed with an electric mixer.

6. In a mixing bowl, combine the eggs and sugar. Beat for 3 to 4 minutes at high speed with an electric mixer, until very thick and lemon colored. Fold in the chocolate mixture and the almonds.

7. Scrape mixture into the prepared pan with the crust. Bake for 1½ hours, until top is brown.

8. Cool the cake in the pan on a wire cooling rack, and then refrigerate until cold. Run a knife around the sides of the pan to release the cake, and then remove the sides of pan. Allow the cheesecake to sit at room temperature for 30 minutes before serving.

VARIATIONS

• Substitute Frangelico or other hazelnut liqueur and roasted hazelnuts for the amaretto and almonds, and substitute pure vanilla extract for the almond extract.

• Substitute Grand Marnier, triple sec, or other orange liqueur for the amaretto, pure orange oil for the almond extract, and ⅔ cup candied orange rind for the almonds.

TIP: BECAUSE CHOCOLATE CAN ABSORB AROMAS AND FLAVORS FROM OTHER FOODS, IT SHOULD ALWAYS BE WRAPPED TIGHTLY AFTER BEING OPENED. STORE CHOCOLATE IN A COOL, DRY PLACE, BUT IT SHOULD NOT BE REFRIGERATED OR FROZEN. IF STORED AT A HIGH TEMPERATURE, THE FAT WILL RISE TO THE SURFACE AND BECOME A WHITISH POWDER CALLED A BLOOM. IT WILL DISAPPEAR, HOWEVER, AS SOON AS THE CHOCOLATE IS MELTED.

CHOCOLATE CARAMEL PECAN PIE

YIELD: 6 TO 8 SERVINGS
ACTIVE TIME: 20 MINUTES
TOTAL TIME: 1¾ HOURS,
INCLUDING COOLING TIME

1½ cups granulated
sugar

½ cup water

1 cup heavy cream

4 tablespoons (½ stick)
unsalted butter, cut into
small pieces

¼ cup bourbon

2 large eggs

1 cup pecan halves,
toasted at 350 degrees
for 5 minutes

4 ounces bittersweet
chocolate, melted

1 9-inch pre-baked pie
shell

Go big, or go home! This decadent pie combines chocolate with crunchy pecans and mellow caramel. The pie can be made 1 day in advance and refrigerated, tightly covered. Bring it to room temperature before serving.

1. In a small saucepan, combine the sugar and water, and cook over medium-high heat, without stirring, until the liquid is golden brown and caramelized. Turn off the heat and add the cream slowly, stirring with a long-handled spoon; it will bubble up at first. Once the cream has been added, cook the caramel over low heat for 2 more minutes. Strain the mixture into a mixing bowl and allow to cool for 10 minutes.

2. Preheat the oven to 400 degrees.

3. Beat the butter, bourbon, and eggs into the caramel and whisk until smooth. Stir in the pecans.

4. Spread the melted chocolate in the bottom of the pie shell and pour the pecan filling over it.

5. Bake for 15 minutes, then reduce the oven to 350 degrees and bake for an additional 15 minutes.

6. Allow the pie to cool on a wire cooling rack until it's room temperature.

VARIATIONS
• Substitute rum or brandy for the bourbon.

• Substitute walnuts, almonds, or pine nuts for the pecans.

TIP: CARAMELIZING SUGAR IS NOT DIFFICULT, BUT ONE PITFALL IS ALLOWING THE SUGAR TO ACTUALLY REACH DARK BROWN BEFORE REMOVING THE PAN FROM THE HEAT. THE LIQUID AND POT ARE VERY HOT BY THE TIME THE SUGAR STARTS TO COLOR, SO TAKE THE PAN OFF THE HEAT WHEN THE SYRUP IS A MEDIUM BROWN; IT WILL CONTINUE TO COOK.

GLUTEN FREE GF

MAPLE MACAROONS

By Alexandra Lewis

MAKES ABOUT TWO DOZEN COOKIES (DEPENDING ON COOKIE SIZE)
ACTIVE TIME: 15 MINUTES
TOTAL TIME: 40 MINUTES

1 14-oz package (about 5 cups) shredded, sweetened coconut

¼ cup maple sugar

¼ cup white sugar

⅛ teaspoon salt

3 egg whites

½ teaspoon maple extract

Not to be confused with the delicate and delightful—but also much more complicated—French macaron, this sweet and simple recipe for maple macaroons puts a sweet spin on the classic, chewy coconut treat. Perfect for capping off a fall feast! (Plus, they're naturally gluten-free.)

1. Preheat oven to 325 degrees and line two baking sheets with parchment paper.

2. In a medium bowl, combine the coconut, sugars, and salt.

3. In a separate bowl, beat the egg whites with an electric mixer on medium-high for about 3 minutes, until soft peaks form.

4. Add the egg mixture and maple extract to the dry ingredients and mix well.

5. Drop the dough by rounded tablespoonfuls onto the parchment-lined baking sheets. Bake for about 20 minutes, until golden brown. Don't overbake or your cookies will be dry rather than chewy.

6. Cool on a wire cooling rack.

CONTRIBUTORS

INDIVIDUAL CONTRIBUTORS

Joshua M. Bernstein

Joshua M. Bernstein is a beer journalist and critic who has written for *New York, Saveur, Details, Time Out New York, Draft, Forbes Traveler, The New York Times,* and Gourmet.com, where he was the beer columnist. He is a contributing editor to the drinks magazine *Imbibe*. He's been featured on NPR's Marketplace and Beer Sessions Radio. His books include *The Complete Beer Course* and *Brewed Awakening*. He lives in Brooklyn, New York.

Warren Bobrow

Warren Bobrow is the author of *Apothecary Cocktails* and *Whiskey Cocktails*, and more than 300 articles on food, wine, and cocktail mixology. In addition to his popular blog, The Cocktail Whisperer, he writes for the Williams-Sonoma blog, Foodista.com, *Voda, Saveur, Serious Eats, The Beverage Journal, Beverage News,* and *Edible New Jersey*. Warren has taught at the New School in New York as well as the Institute for Culinary Education.

Rémy Charest

Québec City–based journalist and translator Rémy Charest has been writing about wine and food for almost twenty years in daily newspapers, magazines, and online publications in Canada and the United States, including *Cellier, WineAlign, enRoute, Le Devoir,* and *Punch Drink*. He also judges at national and international competitions—and travels too much.

Lynne Devereux

Lynne Devereux directs marketing and PR for two California cheese companies, Laura Chenel's Chèvre and Marin French Cheese Company. Her company, Butter Communications, produces targeted marketing and press materials, advertising, and social media communications for specialty food and beverage clients. She created and directed California's Artisan Cheese Festival in Sonoma and was the founding president of the California Artisan Cheese Guild. She has taught classes at the Culinary Institute of America at Greystone and the San Francisco Cheese School, and develops cheese-pairing programs for wineries, brewers, and cider makers.

Carlo DeVito

Carlo DeVito is a wine, beer, cider, and spirits editor and writer with more than 20 years of experience in the book industry. He has worked with some of the most famous chefs, mixologists, and experts in those industries and has appeared on radio and television. He also publishes the blog EastCoastWineries.

Howard G. Goldberg

Howard G. Goldberg was an editor at the *The New York Times* from 1970 to 2004. He began contributing wine articles in the mid-1980s and in 1987, wrote the Wine Talk column for a period. He edited *The New York Times Book of Wine* and wrote *All About Wine Cellars*.

Peter Kaminsky

Peter Kaminsky has written many books about cooking and fly fishing. He offers prime rib recipes in John Madden's *Ultimate Tailgating, Seven Fires: The Argentine Way to Grill* (with Francis Mallmann), and *Mallmann On Fire* (with Francis Mallmann), and *Charred and Scruffed* (with Adam Perry Lang). He is the former managing editor of *National Lampoon*, and his *Outdoors* column has appeared in *The New York Times* for twenty-five years.

Dave McIntyre

Dave McIntyre is the nationally recognized wine columnist for *The Washington Post*. He also blogs at dmwineline.com and is one of the founding members of Drink Local Wine.

Eric Steinman

Eric Steinman is an editor and writer who has been covering food culture and social issues for more than a decade. In 2009, he founded *Edible Hudson Valley*, where he continues to serve as editor-in-chief. In addition, he has spoken on the subject of the evolution of the local food movement in the United States and has taught on the subject at Bard College. He continues to write and report for such publications as *The New York Times, Playboy, Organic Gardening,* and *Bon Appétit.*

Amy E. Zavatto

Food, wine, and spirits maven Amy Zavatto has written for *New York,* Frommers.com, *Imbibe, Edible Brooklyn, Food & Wine, Time Out New York,* and many other newspapers, magazines, and websites. She is the author of *The Architecture of the Cocktail, The Complete Idiot's Guide to Bartending,* and *A Hedonist's Guide to Eat New York.*

FARM CONTRIBUTORS

Glynwood

Cold Spring, NY

glynwood.org

While acting as a working farm and CSA, Glynwood is an educational and advocacy hub helping to train farmers and promote farming and regional food throughout the area. They exist at the forefront of smart and sustainable farming while sharing their knowledge and good fortune with farmers and start-ups throughout the Hudson Valley.

Marin Sun Farms

Point Reyes Station, CA

marinsunfarms.com

Situated in the undeniably picturesque, rolling grasslands of the Point Reyes National Seashore, Marin Sun Farms produces grass-fed and pasture-raised animals utilizing a sustainable food model that conserves the landscape, supports the health of its inhabitants, and restores the vitality of the region. All that with some beautifully raised beef, poultry, pork, lamb, and goat, and you have yourself an ideal farming operation.

McClendon's Select

Peoria, Arizona

mcclendonsselect.com

A Slow Food USA member and third generation family farm run by Bob McClendon and his wife Kate, McClendon's Select provides certified organic citrus, honey, dates, and vegetables to area chefs and farmers' market denizens lucky enough to gather up some of their offerings. For those outside of the area, McClendon's citrus, honey, dates, and organic soap can be ordered online through their website.

Migliorelli Farm

Tivoli, NY

migliorelli.com

Started from a handful of broccoli raab seeds back in the 1930s, the Migliorelli family has built up a healthy and bountiful farm enterprise that brings fresh fruit and produce to the Hudson Valley. Their wide array of products can be had at one of their many farm stands throughout the Hudson Valley, or gathered at the many farmers' markets they operate out of New York City.

Muth Family Farm

Williamstown, NJ

muthfamilyfarm.com

Considered a "master grower," Bob Muth of Muth Family Farm is an agricultural darling of New Jersey's farming community and has gained recognition as one of the leading regional farmers in the area of sustainable agriculture as well as organic farming. The Muth Family Farm runs a well-attended CSA program and produces some of the best tomatoes in the area.

Quail Hill Farm

Amagansett, NY

peconiclandtrust.org/quail_hill_farm.html

Running one of the original CSAs in the nation, Quail Hill Farm is located on 30 plus acres in the East Hampton region of Long Island. It serves 200 families along with countless restaurants, schools, and farmers' markets in the area. Run by "poet farmer" Scott Chaskey, Quail Hill is a unique, rough-hewn jewel amongst the luxury of Eastern Long Island.

Untiedt's Vegetable Farm, Inc.

Waverly, MN

untiedtswegrowforyou.com

Untiedt's Vegetable Farm started back in the 1970s as a riverside farm on a modest 40 acres. This family farm has significantly expanded throughout the decades but maintains strong Minnesota-grown, hand-harvested, and locally centered ideals alongside sustainable practices that produce sweet corn, pumpkins, and squash sold at farmers' markets and their own conspicuous red, green, and yellow gazebos around the region.

INDEX

ABOUT JOHN WHALEN III

John Whalen III has been cooking under the tutelage of such acclaimed chefs as Jonathan Cartwright (Executive Chef of The White Barn Inn in Kennebunkport, ME) since his teenage years. He is also the author of *Paleo Grilling: The Complete Cookbook*.

ABOUT CIDER MILL PRESS BOOK PUBLISHERS

Good ideas ripen with time. From seed to harvest, Cider Mill Press brings fine reading, information, and entertainment together between the covers of its creatively crafted books. Our Cider Mill bears fruit twice a year, publishing a new crop of titles each spring and fall.

VISIT US ON THE WEB AT
www.cidermillpress.com

OR WRITE TO US AT
12 Spring Street
PO Box 454
Kennebunkport, Maine 04046